W9-DBQ-408

American Economic History
Since 1860

GOLDENTREE BIBLIOGRAPHIES
IN AMERICAN HISTORY
under the series editorship of
Arthur S. Link

American Economic History Since 1860

compiled by

Edward C. Kirkland

Bowdoin College

AHM Publishing Corporation
Northbrook, Illinois 60062

Copyright © 1971

AHM PUBLISHING CORPORATION

All rights reserved

This book, or parts thereof, must not be
used or reproduced in any manner without
written permission. For information address
the publisher, AHM PUBLISHING
CORPORATION, 1500 Skokie Boulevard,
Northbrook, Illinois 60062.

ISBN: 0-88295-519-5
(Formerly 390-51231-1)

Library of Congress Card Number: 74-158954

PRINTED IN THE UNITED STATES OF AMERICA

783

Second Printing

Editor's Foreword

GOLDENTREE BIBLIOGRAPHIES IN AMERICAN HISTORY are designed to provide students, teachers, and librarians with ready and reliable guides to the literature of American history in all its remarkable scope and variety. Volumes in the series cover comprehensively the major periods in American history, while additional volumes are devoted to all important subjects.

Goldentree Bibliographies attempt to steer a middle course between the brief list of references provided in the average textbook and the long bibliography in which significant items are often lost in the sheer number of titles listed. Each bibliography is, therefore, selective, with the sole criterion for choice being the significance—and not the age—of any particular work. The result is bibliographies of all works, including journal articles and doctoral dissertations, that are still useful, without bias in favor of any particular historiographical school.

Each compiler is a scholar long associated, both in research and teaching, with the period or subject of his volume. All compilers have not only striven to accomplish the objective of this series but have also cheerfully adhered to a general style and format. However, each compiler has been free to define his field, make his own selections, and work out internal organization as the unique demands of his period or subject have seemed to dictate.

The single great objective of *Goldentree Bibliographies in American History* will have been achieved if these volumes help researchers and students to find their way to the significant literature of American history.

Arthur S. Link

Preface

ANY ARRANGEMENT OF book and periodical titles under topical headings involves arbitrary decisions. In this instance the bibliographer must first decide what economic history is. In view of the continuous debates on the relative attention to be given to economic theory or "models" or to the description of strictly contemporary phenomena, the bibliographer is as soon made aware of the difficulty of definition as he is of the inconclusiveness of an effort to find one. If he assumes economics deals with the production, distribution, and consumption of goods and services and that history must cover a time span of at least a decade—any decade—to be historical, further certainty eludes him in the thickets of methodology. Some scholars prefer to use words to convey meaning; others believe measurement or quantification superior to "mere narration" and "implicit" values. These viewpoints are not as antithetical as many of the disputants imagine.

I have sought to give examples of the better works of various schools of thought and to follow conventional definitions of economics and history. To give full attention to the areas where economic history overlaps with foreign affairs, domestic politics, population growth and distribution, and social phenomena would obviously distend this bibliography into one for American history and culture as a whole. I do not think this would be useful.

In short I have sought to be suggestive and selective. Consequently I have considered it my duty at least to examine the various items in the following list. Hence the bibliography is not exhaustive. Where subject matter overlaps the boundaries of various periods or topics, I hope cross references will provide guide lines. The largest single bloc of items occurs in the middle period—1877 to 1914. This coincidence is not a value judgment; it is an open-ended, and hence convenient, period for the assignment of border-line items. This outcome is perhaps another example of the inevitability of the middle way.

E.C.K.

Abbreviations

Ag Hist	Agricultural History
Am Econ Rev	American Economic Review
Am Hist Rev	American Historical Review
Am J Econ Socio	American Journal of Economics and Sociology
Ann Rep Am Hist Assn	Annual Report of the American Historical Association
Bus Hist Rev	Business History Review
Econ Dev Cult Change	Economic Development and Cultural Change
Explo Entre Hist	Explorations in Entrepreneurial History, 2d Series
Har Bus Rev	Harvard Business Review, Harvard University
Indus Labor Rel Rev	Industrial and Labor Relations Review
J Am Hist	The Journal of American History
J Econ Bus Hist	Journal of Economic and Business History
J Econ Hist	Journal of Economic History
J Mod Hist	Journal of Modern History
J Pol Econ	Journal of Political Economy
J S Hist	Journal of Southern History
Miss Val Hist Rev	Mississippi Valley Historical Review
Ohio Hist Q	Ohio Historical Quarterly
Pac Hist Rev	Pacific Historical Review
Penn History	Pennsylvania History
Pers Am Hist	Perspectives in American History
Pol Sci Q	Political Science Quarterly
Proc Am Philos Soc	Proceedings, American Philosophical Society
Q J Econ	Quarterly Journal of Economics
Rev Econ Stat	Review of Economic Statistics

Note: Cross-references are to page and to item numbers. Items marked by a dagger (†) are available in paperback edition at the time this bibliography goes to press. The publisher and compiler invite suggestions for additions to future editions of the bibilography.

Contents

I. General Trends in the Performance of the Economy

A. Measurements and Definitions

1 ABRAMOVITZ, Moses. "Resource and Output Trends in the United States Since 1870." *Occasional Paper 52*, National Bureau of Economic Research. New York, 1956.

2 BURNS, A. F. *Production Trends in the United States Since 1870*. New York, 1934.

3 FABRICANT, Solomon. "Basic Facts on Productivity Change." *Occasional Paper 63*, National Bureau of Economic Reasearch. New York, 1959.

4 KENDRICK, John W. *Productivity Trends in the United States*. Princeton, 1961.

5 KUZNETS, Simon. *National Product Since 1869*. New York, 1946.

6 KUZNETS, Simon, and Raymond GOLDSMITH. *Income and Wealth of the United States: Trends and Structure*. Papers for the International Association for Research in Income and Wealth. Cambridge, Eng., 1952.

7 KING, W. I. *The Wealth and Income of the People of the United States*. New York, 1915.

8 MARTIN, Robert F. *National Income in the United States, 1799–1938*. New York, 1939.

9 National Bureau of Economic Research. "Output, Employment, and Productivity in the United States." Vol. XXX of *Studies in Income and Wealth*. New York, 1966.

10 National Bureau of Economic Research. "Trends in the American Economy in the Nineteenth Century." Vol. XXIV of *Studies in Income and Wealth*. Princeton, 1960.

11 United States Bureau of the Census. *Historical Statistics of the United States, Colonial Times to 1957*. Washington, D.C., 1960.

B. Economic Vacillations (The Business Cycle)

12 ABRAMOVITZ, Moses. *Evidences of Long Swings in Aggregate Construction Since the Civil War*. New York, 1965.†

13 ABRAMOVITZ, Moses. "Nature and Significance of Kuznets Cycles." *Econ Dev Cult Change*, IX (1961), 225–248.

1 ARIELI, Yehoshua. *Individualism and Nationalism in American Ideology.* Cambridge, Mass., 1964.

2 BURNS, Arthur F. "Progress Towards Economic Stability." *Am Econ Rev,* L (1960), 1–19.

3 FELS, Rendigs. *American Business Cycles, 1865–1897.* Chapel Hill, N.C., 1959.

4 FRICKEY, Edwin. *Economic Fluctuations in the United States: A Systematic Analysis of Long-run Trends and Business Cycles, 1866–1914.* Cambridge, Mass., 1942.

5 KUZNETS, Simon. "Long Swings in the Growth of Population and in Related Economic Variables." *Proc Am Philos Soc,* CII (1958), 25–52.

6 MITCHELL, W. C. *Business Cycles.* Berkeley, 1913.†

7 MITCHELL, W. C. *Business Cycles, The Problem and Its Setting.* New York, 1927.

8 REZNECK, S. *Business Depressions and Financial Panics. Essays in American Business and Economic History.* New York, 1968.

9 SCHUMPETER, J. A. *Business Cycles. A Theoretical, Historical, and Statistical Analysis of the Capitalist Process.* 2 vols. New York and London, 1939, pp. 303–436; 692–904.

10 THORP, Williard L. *Business Annals.* New York, 1926, pp. 107–145.

C.   Factors in Economic Change: Identification and Interpretation

11 ABRAMOVITZ, Moses. "Resource and Output Trends in the United States Since 1870." *Occasional Paper 52,* National Bureau of Economic Research. New York, 1956.

12 COLE, A. H. *Business Enterprise in Its Social Setting.* Cambridge, Mass., 1959.

13 COOTNER, P. H. "The Role of the Railroads in United States Economic Growth." *J Econ Hist,* XXIII (1963), 477–521.

14 DORFMAN, Joseph. *The Economic Mind in American Civilization.* Vols. 3–5. New York, 1946–1959.

15 EASTERLIN, R. A. "The American Baby Boom in Historical Perspective." *Am Econ Rev,* LI (1961), 869–904.

16 FINE, S. A. *Laissez Faire and the General-Welfare State, 1865–1901.* Ann Arbor, Mich., 1956.

17 FOGEL, R. W. *Railroads and American Economic Growth: Essays in Econometric History.* Baltimore, 1964.

18 FRIEDMAN, Milton. "The Role of Monetary Policy." *Am Econ Rev,* LVII (1968), 1–17.

19 FRIEDMAN, Milton, and A. J. SCHWARTZ. *A Monetary History of the United States, 1867–1960.* Princeton, 1963.

1 GOLDSMITH, R. W. *A Study of Saving in the United States*. 3 vols. Princeton, 1955.

2 HURST, J. W. *Law and the Conditions of Freedom*. Madison, Wis., 1956.

3 HURST, J. W. *Law and Social Process in United States History*. Ann Arbor, Mich., 1960.

4 JENKS, L. H. "Railroads as an Economic Force in American Development." *J Econ Hist*, IV (1944), 1–20.

5 JOHNSON, H. G. "Monetary Theory and Policy." *Am Econ Rev*, LII (1962), 337–378.

6 KUZNETS, Simon. *Capital in the American Economy: Its Formation and Financing*. Princeton, 1961.

7 KUZNETS, Simon. *Economic Growth and Structure: Selected Essays*. New York, 1965.

8 KUZNETS, Simon. *Modern Economic Growth: Rate Structure and Spread*. New Haven, Conn., 1966.†

9 KUZNETS, Simon, and Dorothy S. THOMAS, eds. *Population Redistribution and Economic Growth, United States, 1870–1950*. 3 vols. Philadelphia, 1957, 1960.

10 LEBERGOTT, Stanley. *Manpower in Economic Growth: The American Record Since 1800*. New York, 1964.

11 LIPSEY, R. E. *Price and Quantity Trends in the Foreign Trade of the United States*. Princeton, 1963.

12 Mc CLELLAND, P. D. "Railroads, American Growth, and the New Economic History: A Critique." *J Econ Hist*, XXVIII (1968), 102–123.

13 MACHLUP, Fritz. *The Production and Distribution of Knowledge in the United States*. Princeton, 1962.

14 NORTH, D. C. "Economic History: Its Contribution to Economic Education, Research and Policy." *Am Econ Rev Papers and Proceedings*, LV (1965), 86–91.

15 NORTH, D. C. *Growth and Welfare in the American Past—A New Economic History*. Englewood Cliffs, N.J., 1966.†

16 OWEN, Wyn F. "The Double Developmental Squeeze on Agriculture." *Am Econ Rev*, LVI (1966), 43–70.

17 ROSTOW, W. W., ed. *The Economics of Take-off into Sustained Growth. Proceedings of a Conference Held by the International Economic Association.* New York, 1964.

18 SPENGLER, J. J. "The Economist and the Population Question." *Am Econ Rev*, LVI (1966), 1–24.

19 TOBIN, James. "The Monetary Interpretation of History." *Am Econ Rev*, LV (1965), 464–485.

II. Bibliographies on Special Phases or Topics

1 COCHRAN, T. C. "Recent Contributions to Economic History: The United States, the Twentieth Century." *J Econ Hist*, XIX (1959), 64–75.

2 DANIELLS, L. M. *Studies in Enterprise.* Boston, 1957.

3 EDWARDS, E. E. *References on the History of Agriculture in the United States.* Washington, D.C., 1933.

4 FITE, Gilbert C. *American Agriculture and Farm Policy Since 1900.* New York, 1964.

5 FREIDEL, Frank. *The New Deal in Historical Perspective.* Washington, D.C., 1959.

6 GALAMBOS, Louis. *American Business History.* Washington, D.C., 1967.†

7 GATES, P. W. "Research in the History of American Land Tenure." *Ag Hist*, XXVIII (1954), 121–126.

8 GLAAB, C. N. "The History of the American City: Bibliographical Survey." *The Study of Urbanization.* Ed. by D. M. Hauser and L. F. Schnore. New York, 1965.

9 GRANTHAM, D. W., Jr. *The United States Since 1945.* Washington, D.C., 1968.†

10 HUTCHINS, J. G. B. "Recent Contributions to Business History: The United States." *J Econ Hist*, XIX (1959), 103–121.

11 KIRKENDALL, R. S. "The New Deal as Watershed: The Recent Literature." *J Am Hist*, LIV (1968), 839–852.

12 LARSON, H. M. *Guide to Business History.* Cambridge, Mass., 1948.

13 LeDUC, T. "Recent Contributions to Economic History: The United States, 1861–1900." *J Econ Hist*, XIX (1959), 44–63.

14 MOWRY, G. E. *The Progressive Movement, 1900–1920: Recent Ideas and New Literature.* Washington, D.C., 1958.

15 NEUFELD, M. F. *A Representative Bibliography of American Labor History.* Ithaca, N.Y., 1964.

16 ROSE, F. D. *American Labor in Journals of History: A Bibliography.* Champaign, Ill., 1962.

17 ROSS, F. A., and L. V. KENNEDY. *A Bibliography of Negro Migration.* New York, 1934.

18 SAWYER, J. E. "Entrepreneurial Studies. Perspectives and Directions, 1948–1958." *Bus Hist Rev*, XXXII (1958), 434–443.

1 SCHLEIFFER, Hedwig. *Index to Economic History Essays in Festschriften, 1900–1950*. Cambridge, Mass., 1953.

2 STEVENS, H. R. "Recent Writings in Midwestern Economic History." *Ohio Hist Q*, LXIX (1960), 1–31.

3 STROUD, G. S., and G. E. DONAHUE. *Labor History in the United States*. Urbana, Ill., 1961.

4 United States Department of the Interior, Bureau of Land Management. *Public Lands Bibliography*. Washington, D.C., 1962.

III. Civil War and Reconstruction, 1860–1877

A. General Works

5 ANDREANO, Ralph, ed. *The Economic Impact of the American Civil War*. Cambridge, Mass., 1967.†

6 COULTER, E. M. *The Confederate States of America, 1861–1865*. Baton Rouge, 1950.

7 COULTER, E. M. *The South During Reconstruction, 1865–1877*. Baton Rouge, 1947, pp. 184–274.

8 ENGERMAN, S. L. "The Economic Impact of the Civil War." *Explo Entre Hist*, 2d ser., III (1966), 176–199.

9 FITE, E. D. *Social and Industrial Conditions in the North During the Civil War*. New York, 1910.

10 GILCHRIST, D. T., and W. D. LEWIS, eds. *Economic Change in the Civil War Era*. Greenville, Del., 1965.

11 MASSEY, Mary E. *Ersatz in the Confederacy*. Columbia, S.C., 1952.

12 MERK, Frederick. *Economic History of Wisconsin During the Civil War Decade*. Madison, Wis., 1916.

13 MERRITT, R. H. *Engineering in American Society, 1850–1875*. Lexington, Ky., 1969.

14 NEVINS, Allan. *Abram S. Hewitt with Some Account of Peter Cooper*. New York and London, 1935.

15 NEVINS, Allan. *The Emergence of Modern America, 1865–1878*. New York, 1927.

16 NEVINS, Allan. *The War for the Union*. 2 vols. New York, 1959–1960.

17 SCHWAB, J. C. *The Confederate States of America 1861–1865. A Financial and Industrial History of the South During the Civil War*. New York, 1901.

B. Agriculture

1 ABBOTT, Martin. "Free Land, Free Labor, and the Freedmen's Bureau." *Ag Hist*, XXX (1956), 150–156.

2 BROOKS, R. P. *The Agrarian Revolution in Georgia, 1865–1912.* Madison, Wis., 1914.

3 CARTENSEN, Vernon, ed. *The Public Lands: Studies in the History of the Public Domain.* Madison, Wis., 1963.†

4 COULTER, E. M. "The Movement for Agricultural Reorganization in the Cotton South During the Civil War." *Ag Hist*, I (January, 1927), 3–17.

5 DANHOF, C. H. *Change in Agriculture: The Northern United States, 1820–1870.* Cambridge, Mass., 1969.

6 GATES, Paul W. *Agriculture and the Civil War.* New York, 1965.

7 GATES, P. W., and R. W. SWENSON. *History of Public Land Law Development.* Washington, D.C., 1968.

8 JONES, R. L. *Ohio Agriculture During the Civil War.* Columbus, Ohio, 1962.

9 LERNER, E. M. "Southern Output and Agricultural Income, 1860–1880." *Ag Hist*, XXXIII (1959), 117–125.

10 McFEELY, W. S. *Yankee Stepfather: General O. O. Howard and the Freedmen.* New Haven, Conn., and London, 1968.

11 RASMUSSEN, Wayne D. "The Civil War. A Catalyst of Agricultural Revolution." *Ag Hist*, XXXIX (October, 1965), 187–195.

12 SALOUTOS, Theodore. "Southern Agriculture and the Problems of Readjustment: 1865–1877." *Ag Hist*, XXX (1956), 58–76.

13 TILDEN, Arnold. *The Legislation of the Civil War Period Considered as a Basis of the Agricultural Revolution in the United States.* Los Angeles, 1937.

14 WILEY, B. I. *Southern Negroes, 1861–1865.* New Haven, Conn., 1938.†

15 ZEICHNER, Oscar. "The Transition from Slave to Free Agricultural Labor in the Southern States." *Ag Hist*, XIII (1939), 22–32.

C. Manufacturing

16 BRUCE, Kathleen. *Virginia Iron Manufacture in the Slave Era.* New York and London, 1930.

17 DEW, C. B. *Ironmaker to the Confederacy: Joseph R. Anderson and the Tredegar Iron Works.* New Haven, Conn., and London, 1966.

18 HANCOCK, H. B., and N. B. WILKINSON. "A Manufacturer in Wartime: Du Pont, 1860–1865." *Bus Hist Rev*, XL (1966), 213–236.

1   RAMSDELL, C. W. "The Control of Manufacturing by the Confederate Government." *Miss Val Hist Rev*, VIII (1921), 232–249.

D.   Finance, Debt, Money

2   BARRETT, D. C. *The Greenbacks and Resumption of Specie Payments, 1862–1879*. Cambridge, Mass., 1931.

3   DAVIS, A. M. *The Origin of the National Banking System*. Washington, D.C., 1910–1911.

4   DESTLER, C. M. *American Radicalism, 1865–1901*. New London, Conn., 1946.†

5   HAMMOND, Bray. *Sovereignty and an Empty Purse: Banks and Politics in the Civil War*. Princeton, 1970.

6   MITCHELL, W. C. *A History of the Greenbacks with Special Reference to the Economic Consequences of Their Use, 1862–65*. Chicago, 1903.

7   SHARKEY, R. P. *Money, Class and Party. An Economic Study of Civil War and Reconstruction*. Baltimore, 1959.†

8   TODD, R. C. *Confederate Finance*. Athens, Ga., 1954.

9   UNGER, Irwin. *The Greenback Era. A Social and Political History of American Finance, 1865–1879*. Princeton, 1964.

E.   Transportation

10 AMES, C. E. *Pioneering the Union Pacific. A Reappraisal of the Builders of the Railroad*. New York, 1969.

11 BLACK, R. C., III. *The Railroads of the Confederacy*. Chapel Hill, N.C., 1952.

12 FOGEL, R. W. *The Union Pacific Railroad, A Case in Premature Enterprise*. Baltimore, 1960.

13 HENRY, R. S., ed. "Civil War Railroads." *Civil War History*, VII (1961), 229–320.

14 RAMSDELL, C. W. "The Confederate Government and the Railroads." *Am Hist Rev*, XXII (1917), 794–810.

15 RUSSEL, R. R. *Improvement of Communication with the Pacific Coast as an Issue in American Politics, 1783–1864*. Cedar Rapids, Iowa, 1948.

16 SIMKINS, F. B., and R. H. WOODY. *South Carolina During Reconstruction*. Chapel Hill, N.C., 1932.

17 STOVER, J. F. *The Railroads of the South, 1865–1900: A Study in Finance and Control*. Chapel Hill, N.C., 1955.

18 WEBER, Thomas. *The Northern Railroads in the Civil War, 1861–1865*. New York, 1952.

F. Labor

1 ANDREWS, J. B. "Nationalization (1860–1877)." Vol. II of *History of Labour in the United States*, by J. R. Commons et al. New York, 1918.

2 BRANDEIS, Elizabeth. "Labor Legislation." Vol. III of *History of Labor in the United States, 1896–1932*, by J. R. Commons et al. New York, 1935.

3 GROB, G. N. *Workers and Utopia: A Study of Ideological Conflict in the American Labor Movement, 1865–1900*. Evanston, Ill., 1961.†

4 GROSSMAN, J. P. *William Sylvis, Pioneer of American Labor. A Study of the Labor Movement During the Era of Civil War*. New York, 1945.

5 LESCOHIER, D. D. "Working Conditions." Vol. III of *History of Labor in the United States, 1896–1932*, by J. R. Commons et al. New York, 1935.

6 TODES, Charlotte. *William H. Sylvis and the National Labor Union*. New York, 1942.

IV. The Era of Rapid Economic Growth, 1877–1914

A. General Works

7 ALLEN, F. L. *The Big Change, 1900–1950*. New York, 1952.

8 CLARK, T. D. *The Emerging South*. New York, 1968.†

9 DEGLER, C. N. *The Age of the Economic Revolution, 1876–1900*. Glenview, Ill., 1967.

10 GINGER, Ray. *Age of Excess: The United States from 1877 to 1914*. New York, 1965.†

11 HAYS, Samuel P. *The Response to Industralism: 1885–1914*. Chicago, 1957.†

12 HUGHES, Jonathan. *The Vital Few: American Progress and Its Protagonists*. Boston, 1966.

13 JOSEPHSON, Matthew. *The Robber Barons, The Great American Capitalists 1861–1901*. New York, 1934.

14 KIRKLAND, E. C. *Industry Comes of Age. Business, Labor, and Public Policy, 1860–1897*. Chicago, 1967.†

15 MORGAN, H. W., ed. *The Gilded Age: A Reappraisal*. Syracuse, 1963.

16 WEISBERGER, B. R. *The New Industrial Society, 1848–1900*. New York, 1969.

17 WELLS, D. A. *Recent Economic Changes*. New York, 1889.

B. Agriculture

1. GENERAL WORKS

1 BARGER, Harold, and H. H. LANDSBERG. *American Agriculture, 1899–1939. A Study of Output, Employment and Productivity.* New York, 1942.

2 BLACK, J. D., and R. H. ALLEN. "The Growth of Farm Tenancy in the United States." *Q J Econ,* LI (1937), 393–425.

3 BOGUE, Allan G. *Money at Interest: The Farm Mortgage on the Middle Border.* Ithaca, N.Y., 1955.†

4 COX, LaWanda C. "The American Agricultural Wage Earner, 1865–1900: The Emergence of a Modern Labor Problem." *Ag Hist,* XXII (1948), 95–114.

5 COX, LaWanda C. "Tenancy in the United States, 1865–1900. A Consideration of the Agricultural Ladder Hypothesis." *Ag Hist,* XVIII (1944), 97–105.

6 CUMMINGS, Richard O. *The American and His Food: A History of Food Habits in the United States.* Chicago, 1941.

7 DANHOF, C. H. *Change in Agriculture. The Northern United States 1820–1870.* Cambridge, Mass., 1969.

8 ELSWORTH, R. H., and Grace WANSTALL. "Farmers' Marketing and Purchasing Cooperatives, 1863–1939." Farm Credit Administration, Cooperative Research and Service Division, *Miscellaneous Report* No. 40. Washington, D.C., 1941.

9 FITE, G. C. *The Farmers' Frontier, 1865–1900.* New York, 1966.

10 GOLDENWEISER, E. A., and L. E. TRUESDELL. *Farm Tenancy in the United States.* Census Monographs, IV. Washington, D.C., 1924.

11 IWATA, Masakazu. "The Japanese Immigrants in California Agriculture." *Ag Hist,* XXXVI (1962), 26–37.

12 JOHNSTONE, P. H. "Old Ideals Versus New Ideas in Farm Life." *Farmers in a Changing World: The Yearbook of Agriculture, 1940.* U.S. Department of Agriculture, Washington, D.C., 1940, pp. 141–167.

13 PETERSON, A. G. "Futures Trading with Particular Reference to Agricultural Commodities." *Ag Hist,* VII (1933), 68–80.

14 SHANNON, F. A. *The Farmers' Last Frontier, Agriculture, 1860–1897.* New York, 1945.†

15 SHU-CHING LEE, "The Theory of the Agricultural Ladder," *Ag Hist,* XXI (1947), 53–61.

2. CROPS AND REGIONS

a. Cereals

16 ARRINGTON, L. J. *Great Basin Kingdom. An Economic History of the Latter-Day Saints, 1830–1900.* Cambridge, Mass., 1958.†

1 BALL, C. R. "The History of American Wheat Improvement." *Ag Hist*, IV (1930), 48–71.

2 BATEMAN, Fred. "Improvement in American Dairy Farming, 1850–1910: A Quantitative Analysis." *J Econ Hist*, XXVIII (1968), 255–273.

3 BOGUE, Allan G. *From Prairie to Corn Belt. Farming in Illinois and Iowa Prairies in the Nineteenth Century.* Chicago, 1963.†

4 DRACHE, Hiram M. *The Day of the Bonanza: A History of Bonanza Farming in the Red River Valley of the North.* Institute for Regional Studies (N. D.), Fargo, N.D., 1964.

5 HARGREAVES, M. W. M. *Dry Farming in the Northern Great Plains.* Cambridge, Mass., 1957.

6 HICKS, J. D. "The Western Middle West, 1900–1914." *Ag Hist*, XX (1946), 65–77.

7 JARCHOW, M. E. *The Earth Brought Forth: A History of Minnesota Agriculture to 1885.* St. Paul, 1949.

8 LARSON, H. M. *The Wheat Market and the Farmer in Minnesota, 1858–1900.* New York, 1926.

9 LEE, G. A. "The Historical Significance of the Chicago Grain Elevator System." *Ag Hist*, XI (1937), 16–32.

10 MALIN, James C. *Winter Wheat in the Golden Belt of Kansas.* Lawrence, Kan., 1944.

11 OTTOSON, H. W., E. M. BIRCH, P. A. HENDERSON, and A. H. ANDERSON. *Land and People in the Northern Plains Transition Area.* Lincoln, Neb., 1966.

12 REFSELL, O. N. "The Farmers' Elevator Movement." *J Pol Econ*, XXII (1914), 872–895, 969–991.

13 SCHAFER, Joseph. *A History of Agriculture in Wisconsin.* Madison, Wis., 1922.

14 TAYLOR, C. H., ed. *History of the Board of Trade of the City of Chicago.* 3 vols. Chicago, 1917.

15 THOMPSON, J. G. *The Rise and Decline of the Wheat Growing Industry in Wisconsin.* Madison, Wis., 1909.

b. Livestock

16 ATHERTON, Lewis E. *The Cattle Kings.* Bloomington, Ind., 1961.

17 CLELAND, R. G. *The Cattle on a Thousand Hills, Southern California, 1850–1870.* San Marino, Calif., 1941.

18 DALE, Edward E. *The Range Cattle Industry.* Norman, Okla., 1930.

19 EDWARDS, E. E. "Europe's Contribution to the American Dairy Industry." *J Econ Hist*, Supplement, IX (1949), 72–84.

11

1 FRINK, Maurice, W. T. JACKSON, and Agnes W. SPRING. *When Grass Was King*. Boulder, Colo., 1956.

2 GATES, P. W. "Cattle Kings in the Prairies." *Miss Val Hist Rev*, XXXV (1948), 379–412.

3 LAMPARD, Eric E. *The Rise of the Dairy Industry in Wisconsin: A Study in Agricultural Change. 1820–1920*. Madison, Wis., 1963.

4 MOSK, S. A. "Land Policy and Stock Raising in the Western United States." *Ag Hist*, XVII (1943), 14–30.

5 OLIPHANT, J. O. *On the Cattle Ranges of the Oregon Country*. Seattle, 1968.

6 OSGOOD, E. S. *The Day of the Cattleman*. Minneapolis, 1929.†

7 PELZER, Louis. "Financial Management of the Cattle Ranges." *J Econ Bus Hist*, II (1929–30), 723–741.

8 WEBB, Walter P. *The Great Plains*. Boston, 1931.†

c. The South: Cotton, Tobacco, and Sugar

9 BENTLEY, George R. *A History of the Freedmen's Bureau*. Philadelphia, 1955.

10 CLARK, T. D. *Pills, Petticoats and Plows. The Southern Country Store*. Indianapolis and New York, 1944.

11 COHN, David L. *The Life and Times of King Cotton*. New York, 1956.

12 SITTERSON, J. C. *Sugar Country. The Cane Sugar Industry in the South, 1753–1950*. Lexington, Ky., 1953.

13 STREET, James H. *The New Revolution in the Cotton Economy*. Chapel Hill, N.C., 1957.

14 TAYLOR, R. H. "The Sale and Application of Commercial Fertilizers in the South Atlantic States to 1900." *Ag Hist*, XXI (1947), 46–52.

15 TILLEY, N. M. *The Bright Tobacco Industry, 1860–1929*. Chapel Hill, N.C., 1948.

16 TINDALL, G. B. *South Carolina Negroes: 1877–1900*. Columbia, S.C., 1952†.

17 VANCE, R. B. *Human Geography of the South: A Study in Regional Resources and Human Adequacy*. Chapel Hill, N.C., 1932.

18 WHARTON, V. L. *The Negro in Mississippi, 1865–1890*. Chapel Hill, N.C., 1947.†

19 WILEY, B. I. "Salient Changes in Southern Agriculture Since the Civil War." *Ag Hist*, XIII (1939), 64–76.

20 WOODMAN, Harold D. *King Cotton and His Retainers*. Lexington, Ky., 1968.

21 WOODWARD, C. Vann. *Origins of the New South, 1877–1913*. Baton Rouge, 1951.†

3. GOVERNMENT AND AGRICULTURE

a. Land Policy

1 CARTENSEN, Vernon, ed. *The Public Lands: Studies in the History of the Public Domain.* Madison, Wis., 1962.†

2 CURTI, Merle. *The Making of an American Community.* Stanford, 1959.†

3 DECKER, Leslie E. *Railroads, Lands, and Politics: The Taxation of Railroad Land Grants, 1864–1897.* Providence, 1964.

4 DONALDSON, Thomas. *The Public Domain, Its History with Statistics.* Washington, D.C., 1884.

5 DUNHAM, H. H. *Government Handout. A Study in the Administration of the Public Lands, 1875–1891.* Ann Arbor, Mich., 1941.

6 GANOE, J. T. "The Beginnings of Irrigation in the United States." *Miss Val Hist Rev*, XXV (1938–39), 59–78.

7 GANOE, J. T. "The Desert Land Act in Operation, 1877–1891." *Ag Hist*, XI (1937), 142–157.

8 GANOE, J. T. "The Desert Land Act Since 1891." *Ag Hist*, XI (1937), 266–277.

9 GATES, Paul W. "The Homestead Law in Iowa." *Ag Hist*, XXXVIII (1964), 67–78.

10 GATES, Paul W. *The Wisconsin Pine Lands of Cornell University.* Ithaca, N.Y., 1943.

11 GATES, Paul W., and R. W. SWENSON. *History of Public Land Development*, see 6.7.

12 HIBBARD, B. H. *A History of the Public Land Policies.* New York, 1924.†

13 HUFFMAN, Roy E. *Irrigation Development and Public Water Policy.* New York, 1953.

14 JORGENSON, Lloyd P. "Agricultural Expansion into the Semiarid Lands of the West North Central States During the First World War." *Ag Hist*, XXIII (1949), 30–40.

15 LEDUC, Thomas. "Public Policy, Private Investment, and Land Use in American Agriculture, 1825–1875." *Ag Hist*, XXXVII (1963), 3–9.

16 LEDUC, Thomas. "State Disposal of the Agricultural College Land Scrip." *Ag Hist*, XXVIII (1954), 99–107.

17 LEMMER, G. F. *Norman J. Colman and Colman's Rural World.* Columbia, Mo., 1953.

18 MEAD, Elwood. *Irrigation Institutions. A Discussion of the Economic and Legal Questions Created by the Growth of Irrigated Agriculture in the West.* New York, 1903.

1 PEFFER, E. L. *The Closing of the Public Domain: Disposal and Reservation Policies, 1900–1950.* Stanford, 1951.

2 ROBBINS, R. M. *Our Landed Heritage, The Public Domain, 1776–1936.* Princeton, 1942.

3 VON NARDROFF, Ellen. "The American Frontier as a Safety Valve— The Life, Death, Reincarnation, and Justification of a Theory." *Ag Hist*, XXXVI (1962), 123–142.

b. Research and Education

4 BAILEY, Joseph C. *Seaman A. Knapp: Schoolmaster of American Agriculture.* New York, 1945.

5 BENEDICT, Murray R. *Farm Policies of the United States, 1790–1950: A Study of Their Origins and Development.* New York, 1953.

6 COLMAN, Gould P. *Education and Agriculture. A History of the New York State College of Agriculture at Cornell University.* Ithaca, N.Y., 1963.

7 CURTI, Merle, and Vernon CARSTENSEN. *The University of Wisconsin: A History, 1848–1925.* 2 vols. Madison, Wis., 1949.

8 ELLSWORTH, Clayton S. "Theodore Roosevelt's Country Life Commission." *Ag Hist*, XXXIV (1960), 155–172.

9 FAIRCHILD, D. G. *The World Was My Garden: Travels of a Plant Explorer.* New York, 1938.

10 GAUS, John M., and L. O. WOLCOTT. *Public Administration and the United States Department of Agriculture.* Chicago, 1940.

11 HARDING, T. S. *Two Blades of Grass: A History of Scientific Development in the U.S. Department of Agriculture.* Norman, Okla., 1947.

12 HOWARD, L. O. *Fighting the Insects.* New York, 1933.

13 McCALL, A. G. "The Development of Soil Science." *Ag Hist*, V (1931), 43–56.

14 MALIN, J. C. "The Background of the First Bills to Establish a Bureau of Markets, 1911–1912." *Ag Hist*, VI (1932), 107–129.

15 NASH, Gerald D. *State Government and Economic Development: A History of Administrative Policies in California, 1879–1933.* Berkeley Institute of Governmental Studies. Berkeley, 1964.

16 ROSENBERG, Charles E. "The Adams Act: Politics and the Cause of Scientific Research." *Ag Hist*, XXXVIII (1964), 3–12.

17 ROSS, E. D. *Democracy's College: The Land Grant Movement in the Formative Stage.* Ames, Iowa, 1942.

18 ROSS, E. D. *A History of the Iowa State College of Agriculture and Mechanic Arts.* Ames, Iowa, 1942.

19 ROSS, E. D. "The United States Department of Agriculture During the Commissionership . . . 1862–1889." *Ag Hist*, XX (1946), 129–143.

1 RYERSON, K. A. "History and Significance of the Foreign Plant Introduction Work of the United States Department of Agriculture." *Ag Hist*, VII (1933), 110–128.

2 SIMON, John Y. "The Politics of the Morrill Act." *Ag Hist*, XXXVII (1963), 103–111.

3 TOWNE, Jackson E. "President Draper Gets a College of Agriculture in Spite of Himself." *Ag Hist*, XXXVI (1962), 207–212.

4 TRUE, A. C. *A History of Agricultural Experimentation and Research in the United States, 1607–1925, Including a History of the United States Department of Agriculture.* Washington, D.C., 1937.

5 TRUE, A. C. *A History of Agricultural Education in the United States, 1785–1925.* Washington, D.C., 1929.

6 United States Department of Agriculture, Agricultural History Branch. *Century of Service. The First 100 Years of the United States Department of Agriculture.* Washington, D.C., 1963.

7 WOODWARD, C. R. "Woodrow Wilson's Agricultural Philosophy." *Ag Hist*, XIV (1940), 129–142.

4. AGRICULTURE AND MECHANIZATION

8 DANHOF, C. H. "Gathering the Grass." *Ag Hist*, XXX (1956), 169–173.

9 FITE, Gilbert C. "Recent Progress in the Mechanization of Cotton Production in the United States." *Ag Hist*, XXIV (1950), 19–28.

10 ROGIN, Leo. *The Introduction of Farm Machinery in Its Relation to the Productivity of Labor in the Agriculture of the United States During the Nineteenth Century.* Berkeley, 1931.

11 SPENCE, C. C. "Experiments in American Steam Cultivation." *Ag Hist*, XXXIII (1959), 107–116.

12 WIK, R. M. "Henry Ford's Tractors and American Agriculture." *Ag Hist*, XXXVIII (1964), 79–86.

13 WIK, R. M. *Steam Power on the American Farm.* Philadelphia, 1953.

5. AGRICULTURAL ORGANIZATIONS

14 BAHMER, R. H. "The American Society of Equity." *Ag Hist*, XIV (1940), 33–63.

15 BARRETT, C. S. *The Mission, History and Times of the Farmers' Union.* Nashville, Tenn., 1909.

16 BUCK, S. J. *The Granger Movement: A Study of Agricultural Organization and Its Political, Economic and Social Manifestations, 1870–1880.* Cambridge, Mass., 1913.†

1 HICKS, J. D. *The Populist Revolt: A History of the Farmers' Alliance and the People's Party.* Minneapolis, 1931.†

2 HIRSCH, A. H. "Efforts of the Grange in the Middle West to Control the Price Machinery, 1870–1880." *Miss Val Hist Rev*, XV (1929), 473–496.

3 KILE, O. M. *The Farm Bureau Movement.* New York, 1921.

4 KNAPP, J. G. *The Rise of American Cooperative Enterprise, 1620–1920.* Danville, Ill., 1969.

5 LARSEN, G. H., and H. E. ERDMAN. "Aaron Sapiro: Genius of Farm Co-operative Promotion." *Miss Val Hist Ref*, XLIX (1962), 242–268.

6 POLLACK, Norman. *The Populist Response to Industrial America.* Cambridge, Mass., 1962.

7 POWELL, G. H. *Cooperation in Agriculture.* New York, 1913.

8 SALOUTOS, Theodore, and J. D. HICKS. *Agricultural Discontent in the Middle West, 1900–1939.* Madison, Wis., 1951.†

9 TAYLOR, Carl C. *The Farmers Movement, 1620–1920.* New York, 1953.

10 TONTZ, Robert L. "Memberships of General Farmers' Organizations, United States, 1874–1960." *Ag Hist*, XXXVIII (1964), 143–156.

11 WOODMAN, Harold D. "Chicago Businessmen and the 'Granger' Laws." *Ag Hist*, XXXVI (1962), 16–24.

C. Transportation

1. GENERAL WORKS

12 GILCHRIST, D. T. "Albert Fink and the Pooling System." *Bus Hist Rev*, XXXIV (1960), 24–49.

13 GRODINSKY, Julius. *The Iowa Pool: A Study in Railroad Competition, 1870–1884.* Chicago, 1950.

14 HUNT, E. M. "Railroad Social Saving in Nineteenth Century America." *Am Econ Rev*, LVIII (1967), 909–910.

15 O' CONNELL, W. E., Jr. "The Development of the Private Railroad Freight Car, 1830–1966." *Bus Hist Rev*, XLIV (1970), 190–209.

16 STOVER, John F. *American Railroads.* Chicago, 1961.†

17 STOVER, John F. *The Life and Decline of the American Railroad.* New York, 1970.

18 TAYLOR, G. R., and I. D. NEU. *The American Railroad Network: 1861–1890.* Cambridge, Mass., 1956.

19 United States, Industrial Commission. *Report of the Industrial Commission on Transportation.* Vols. IV and IX. Washington, D.C., 1901.

1 WHITE, J. H., Jr. *American Locomotives: An Engineering History, 1830–1880*. Baltimore, 1968.

2. RAILROADS: REGIONAL STUDIES

2 BAKER, G. P. *The Formation of the New England Railroad Systems: A Study of Railroad Combination in the Nineteenth Century*. Cambridge, Mass., 1937.

3 BAUGHMAN, J. P. "The Evolution of Rail-Water Systems of Transportation in the Gulf Southwest, 1836–1890." *J S Hist*, XXXIV (1968), 357–381.

4 BAUGHMAN, J. P. *Charles Morgan and the Development of Southern Transportation*. Nashville, Tenn., 1968.

5 BELCHER, W. W. *The Economic Rivalry Between St. Louis and Chicago 1850–1880*. New York, 1947.

6 CLARK, I. G. *Then Came the Railroads. The Century from Steam to Diesel in the Southwest*. Norman, Okla., 1958.

7 CURRY, L. P. *Rail Routes South*. Lexington, Ky., 1969.

8 GLAAB, C. N. *Kansas City and the Railroads: Community Policy in the Growth of a Regional Metropolis*. Madison, Wis., 1962.

9 GRODINSKY, Julius. *Transcontinental Railway Strategy, 1869–1893*. Philadelphia, 1962.

10 KIRKLAND, E. C. *Men, Cities and Transportation: A Study in New England History, 1820–1900*. 2 vols. Cambridge, Mass., 1948.

11 KLEIN, M. *The Great Richmond Terminal*. Charlottesville, Va., 1970.

12 KLEIN, M. "The Strategy of Southern Railroads." *Am Hist Rev*, LXXIII (1968), 1052–1068.

13 LAMBIE, J. T. *From Mine to Market: The History of Coal Transportation on the Norfolk and Western Railway*. New York, 1954.

14 RIEGEL, R. E. *The Story of the Western Railroads*. New York, 1926.†

15 RUSSEL, R. R. *Improvement of Communication with the Pacific Coast as an Issue in American Politics, 1783–1864*. Cedar Rapids, Iowa, 1948.

16 STOVER, John F. *The Railroads of the South 1865–1900. A Study in Finance and Control*. Chapel Hill, N.C., 1955.

17 WINTHER, O. O. *The Transportation Frontier. Trans-Mississippi West, 1865–1890*. New York, 1964.

3. RAILROADS: INDIVIDUAL ENTERPRISES

18 ADAMS, C. F., Jr., and Henry ADAMS. *Chapters of Erie and Other Essays*. New York, 1886.†

1   ATHEARN, R. G. *Rebel of the Rockies. A History of the Denver and Rio Grande Western Railroad.* New Haven, Conn., and London, 1962.

2   BEAVER, R. C. *The Bessemer and Lake Erie Railroad, 1869–1969.* San Marino, Cal., 1969.

3   BOGEN, J. I. *The Anthracite Railroads.* New York, 1927.

4   BORAK, A. M. "The Chicago, Milwaukee, and St. Paul Railroad." *J Econ Bus Hist*, III (1930), 81–117.

5   BRAYER, H. O. Vol. II of *William Blackmore, Early Financing of the Denver & Rio Grande Railway and Ancillary Land Companies, 1871–1878.* 2 vols. Denver, 1949.

6   BURGESS, G. H., and M. C. KENNEDY. *Centennial History of the Pennsylvania Railroad Company.* Philadelphia, 1949.

7   DAGGETT, Stuart. *Chapters on the History of the Southern Pacific.* New York, 1922.

8   DAGGETT, Stuart. *Railroad Reorganization.* Boston and New York, 1908.

9   DERRICK, S. M. *Centennial History of South Carolina Railroad.* Columbia, S.C., 1930.

10   DOZIER, H. D. *A History of the Atlantic Coast Line Railroad.* Boston and New York, 1920.

11   MOTT, E. H. *Between the Ocean and the Lakes. The Story of Erie.* New York, 1901.

12   OVERTON, R. C. *Burlington Route, a History of the Burlington Lines.* New York, 1965.

13   OVERTON, R. C. *Gulf to Rockies: The Heritage of the Fort Worth and Denver-Colorado and Southern Railways, 1861–1898.* Austin, 1953.

4. RAILROAD LEADERS

14   COCHRAN, T. C. *Railroad Leaders, 1845–1890.* Cambridge, Mass., 1953.

15   ECKENRODE, H. J., and P. W. EDMUNDS. *E. H. Harriman: The Little Giant of Wall Street.* New York, 1933.

16   GRODINSKY, Julius. *Jay Gould: His Business Career, 1867–1892.* Philadelphia, 1957.

17   HEDGES, J. B. *Henry Villard and the Railways of the Northwest.* New Haven, Conn., 1930.

18   HIRSHSON, S. P. *Grenville M. Dodge, Soldier, Politician, Railroad Pioneer.* Bloomington, Ind., 1967.

19   JOHNSON, A. M., and B. E. SUPPLE. *Boston Capitalists and Western Railroads. A Study in the Nineteenth-Century Railroad Investment Process.* Cambridge, Mass., 1967.

1 KIRKLAND, E. C. *Charles Francis Adams, Jr., 1835–1915. The Patrician at Bay.* Cambridge, Mass., 1965.

2 KLEIN, M. "Southern Railroad Leaders, 1865–1893: Identities and Ideologies." *Bus Hist Rev,* XLIII (1968), 288–310.

3 LANE, W. J. *Commodore Vanderbilt, An Epic of the Steam Age.* New York, 1942.

4 LARSON, H. M. *Jay Cooke, Private Banker.* Cambridge, Mass., 1936.

5 LEWIS, Oscar. *The Big Four: The Story of Huntington, Stanford, Hopkins and Crocker and of the Building of the Central Pacific.* New York and London, 1938.

6 NEU, I. D. *Erastus Corning: Merchant and Financier, 1794–1872.* Ithaca, N.Y., 1960.

7 OBERHOLTZER, E. P. *Jay Cooke, Financier of the Civil War.* 2 vols. Philadelphia, 1907.

8 PEARSON, H. G. *An American Railroad Builder, John Murray Forbes.* Boston and New York, 1911.

5. THE GOVERNMENT AND RAILROADS: PROMOTIONAL PHASE

9 GATES, P. W. *The Illinois Central Railroad and Its Colonization Work.* Cambridge, Mass., 1934.

10 GATES, P. W. "The Railroad Land-Grant Legend." *J Econ Hist,* XIV (1954), 143–146.

11 HANEY, L. H. *A Congressional History of Railways in the United States, 1850–1887.* 2 vols. Madison, Wis., 1908–1910.

12 HEDGES, J. B. "The Colonization Work of the Northern Pacific Railroad." *Miss Val Hist Rev,* XIII (1926), 311–342.

13 HENRY, R. S. "The Railroad Land Grant Legend in American History Texts." *Miss Val Hist Rev,* XXXII (1945), 171–194. "Comments on Henry's Article." *Ibid.,* 557–576.

14 MILLION, J. W. *State Aid to Railways in Missouri.* Chicago, 1896.

15 MURRAY, S. N. "Railroads and the Agricultural Development of the Red River Valley of the North, 1870–1890." *Ag Hist,* XXXI (October, 1957), 57–66.

16 OVERTON, R. C. *Burlington West: A Colonization History of the Burlington Railroad.* Cambridge, Mass., 1941.

17 PIERCE, H. H. *Railroads of New York, A Study of Government Aid, 1826–1875.* Cambridge, Mass., 1953.

18 SANBORN, J. B. *Congressional Grants of Land in Aid of Railways.* Madison, Wis., 1899.

19 THRONE, Mildred. "Suggested Research on Railroad Aid to the Farmer, with Particular Reference to Iowa and Kansas." *Ag Hist,* XXXI (October, 1957), 50–56.

6. WATER TRANSPORTATION

1 DIXON, F. H. *A Traffic History of the Mississippi River System.* Washington, D.C., 1909.

2 GJERSET, Knut. *Norwegian Sailors on the Great Lakes: A Study in the History of American Inland Transportation.* Northfield, Minn., 1928.

3 GOODRICH, Carter. *Government Promotion of American Canals and Railroads, 1800–1890.* New York, 1960.

4 GOODRICH, Carter, ed. *Canals and American Economic Development.* New York and London, 1961.

5 HARTSOUGH, M. L. *From Canoe to Steel Barge on the Upper Mississippi.* Minneapolis, 1934.

6 HATCHER, H. H. *Lake Erie.* Indianapolis and New York, 1945.

7 HUNTER, L. C. *Steamboats on the Western Rivers.* Cambridge, Mass., 1949.

8 HUTCHINS, J. G. B. *The American Maritime Industries and Public Policy, 1789–1914.* Cambridge, Mass., 1941.

9 LASS, W. E. *A History of Steamboating on the Upper Missouri River.* Lincoln, Neb., 1962.

10 LEMLY, J. H. "The Mississippi River: St. Louis' Friend or Foe." *Bus Hist Rev*, XXXIX (1965), 7–15.

11 PUTNAM, J. W. *The Illinois and Michigan Canal. A Study in Economic History.* Chicago, 1918.

12 SANDERLIN, W. S. *The Great National Project: A History of the Chesapeake and Ohio Canal.* Baltimore, 1946.

13 United States Bureau of the Census. *Transportation by Water, 1906.* Washington, D.C., 1908.

14 United States Bureau of the Census. *Transportation by Water, 1916.* Washington, D.C., 1920.

15 WILLOUGHBY, William R. *The St. Lawrence Seaway. A Study in Politics and Diplomacy.* Madison, Wis., 1961.

16 WRIGHT, R. J. *Freshwater Whales. A History of the American Ship Building Company and Its Predecessors.* Kent, Ohio, 1969.

D. Industrial Advance

1. GENERAL WORKS

17 AITKIN, H. G. J. *Taylorism at Watertown Arsenal. Scientific Management in Action, 1908–1915.* Cambridge, Mass., 1960.

1 BACKMAN, Jules. *The Economics of the Electrical Machinery Industry.* New York, 1962.

2 BIRR, K. A. "Science in American Industry." *Science and Society in the United States.* Ed. by D. D. Van Tassel and M. G. Hall. Homewood, Ill., 1966.

3 BLICKSILVER, Jack. *Cotton Manufacturing in the Southeast.* Atlanta, 1959.

4 BRIGHT, A. A., Jr. *The Electric-Lamp Industry. Technological Change and Economic Development from 1800 to 1947.* New York, 1949.

5 BROEHL, W. G., Jr. *Precision Valley: The Machine Tool Companies of Springfield, Vermont.* Englewood Cliffs, N.J., 1959.

6 CALLAHAN, R. E. *Education and the Cult of Efficiency: A Study of the Social Forces That Have Shaped the Administration of the Public Schools.* Chicago, 1962.

7 CALVERT, M. A. *The Mechanical Engineer in America 1830–1910.* Baltimore, 1967.

8 CLARK, V. S. *History of Manufactures in the United States, 1860–1914.* Washington, D.C., 1929.

9 COLE, A. H. *The American Wool Manufacture.* 2 vols. Cambridge, Mass., 1926.

10 CONDIT, C. W. *American Building: Materials and Techniques from the Beginning of the First Colonial Settlements to the Present.* Chicago, 1968.

11 COPLEY, F. B. *Frederick W. Taylor, Father of Scientific Management.* 2 vols. New York, 1923.

12 DALE, Ernest, and Charles MELOY. "Hamilton MacFarland Barksdale and the DuPont Contributions to Systematic Management." *Bus Hist Rev,* XXXVI (1962), 127–152.

13 FABRICANT, Solomon. *The Output of Manufacturing Industries. 1899–1937.* New York, 1940.

14 GARVER, F. B., F. M. BOODY, and A. J. NIXON. *The Location of Manufactures in the United States, 1899–1929.* Minneapolis, 1933.

15 GIBB, G. S. *The Saco-Lowell Shops; Textile Machinery Building in New England, 1813–1949.* Cambridge, Mass., 1950.

16 GIEDION, Siegfried. *Mechanization Takes Command.* New York, 1948.

17 HABER, Samuel. *Efficiency and Uplift: Scientific Management in the Progressive Era, 1890–1920.* Chicago, 1964.

18 HAYS, Samuel P. *Conservation and the Gospel of Efficiency: The Progressive Conservation Movement, 1890–1920.* Cambridge, Mass., 1959.†

19 HUNT, E. E., ed. *Scientific Management Since Taylor, A Collection of Authoritative Papers.* New York, 1924.

1 KNOWLTON, E. H. *Pepperell's Progress: History of a Cotton Textile Company, 1844–1945.* Cambridge, Mass., 1948.

2 LINCOLN, S. B. *Lockwood Greene. The History of an Engineering Business, 1832–1958.* Brattleboro, Vt., 1960.

3 Mc DONALD, Forrest. *Let There Be Light, The Electric Utility Industry in Wisconsin, 1881–1955.* Madison, Wis., 1957.

4 MAC LAURIN, W. R. *Invention and Innovation in the Radio Industry.* New York, 1949.

5 MILLER, R. C. *Kilowatts at Work. A History of the Detroit Edison Company.* Detroit, 1958.

6 MITCHELL, Broadus. *The Rise of Cotton Mills in the South.* Baltimore, 1921.

7 MITCHELL, Broadus and G. S. *The Industrial Revolution in the South.* Baltimore, 1930.

8 National Bureau of Economic Research. *The Rate and Direction of Inventive Activity, Economic and Social Factors.* Princeton, 1962.

9 NAVIN, T. R. *The Whitin Machine Works Since 1831.* Cambridge, Mass., 1950.

10 NORTH, D. C. "Industrialization in the United States." In *Cambridge Economic History of Europe,* Vol. VI, pt. 2. Cambridge, Eng., 1965, pp. 673–705.

11 PASSER, H. C. *The Electrical Manufacturers, 1865–1900: A Study in Competition, Entrepreneurship, Technical Change and Economic Growth.* Cambridge, Mass., 1953.

12 RAE, J. B. *American Automobile Manufacturers. The First Forty Years.* Philadelphia, 1959.

13 STRASSMANN, W. Paul. *Risk and Technological Innovation: American Manufacturing Methods During the Nineteenth Century.* Ithaca, N.Y., 1959.

14 TAYLOR, Arthur R. "Loss to the Public in the Insull Collapse: 1932–1946." *Bus Hist Rev,* XXXVI (1962), 188–205.

15 TAYLOR, F. W. *The Principles of Scientific Management.* New York and London, 1911.†

16 TEMIN, Peter. *Iron and Steel in Nineteenth Century America. An Economic Inquiry.* Cambridge, Mass., 1964.

17 THOMPSON, R. L. *Wiring a Continent: The History of the Telegraph Industry in the United States, 1832–1866.* Princeton, 1947.

18 THORP, W. L. *The Integration of Industrial Operation.* Census (1920) Monographs III. Washington, D.C., 1924.

19 WILLIAMSON, H. F. *Winchester, the Gun That Won the West.* Washington, D.C., 1952.

2. *NATURAL RESOURCES*

20 BARGER, Harold, and S. H. SCHURR. *The Mining Industries, 1899–1939. A Study of Output, Employment and Productivity.* New York, 1944.

1 EAVENSON, H. N. *The First Century and a Quarter of American Coal Industry*. Pittsburgh, 1942.

2 GATES, W. B. *Michigan Copper and Boston Dollars: An Economic History of the Michigan Copper Mining Industry*. Cambridge, Mass., 1951.

3 GIDDENS, P. H. *The Birth of the Oil Industry*. New York, 1938.

4 GIDDENS, P. H. *Early Days of Oil*. Princeton, 1948.

5 HIDY, R. W. and M. E. *History of Standard Oil Company* (*New Jersey*). New York, 1955.

6 HIDY, R. W., F. E. HILL, and Allan NEVINS. *Timber and Men: The Weyerhaeuser Story*. New York, 1963.

7 ISE, John. *The United States Forest Policy*. New Haven, Conn., 1920.

8 JONES, Eliot. *The Anthracite Coal Combination in the United States*. Cambridge, Mass., 1914.

9 KUHLMANN, C. B. *The Development of the Flour-Milling Industry in the United States, with Special Reference to the Industry in Minneapolis*. Boston and New York, 1929.

10 LARSON, H. M., and K. W. PORTER. *History of Humble Oil and Refining Company: A Study in Industrial Growth*. New York, 1959.

11 PARSONS, A. B., ed. *Seventy-Five Years of Progress in the Mineral Industry, 1871–1946*. New York, 1948.

12 RICKMAN, Nellie. *Mississippi Harvest: Lumbering in the Longleaf Pine Belt. 1850–1915*. University, Miss., 1962.

13 TARBELL, I. M. *The History of the Standard Oil Company*. New York, 1904.

14 WHITE, G. T. *Formative Years in the Far West: A History of Standard Oil Company of California and Predecessors Through 1919*. New York, 1962.

15 WILLIAMSON, H. F., and A. R. DAUM. *The American Petroleum Industry, 1859–1959*. 2 vols. Evanston, Ill., 1959, 1963.

16 WIRTH, F. P. *The Discovery and Exploitation of the Minnesota Iron Lands*. Cedar Rapids, Iowa, 1937.

3. BUSINESS LEADERS

17 ALLEN, F. L. *The Lords of Creation*. New York and London, 1935.

18 BRIDGES, Hal. *Iron Millionaire. Life of Charlemagne Tower*. Philadelphia, 1952.

19 BRIDGES, Hal. "The Robber Baron Concept in American History." *Bus Hist Rev*, XXXII (1958), 1–13.

20 DESTLER, C. M. "Entrepreneurial Leadership Among the 'Robber Barons': A Trial Balance." *J Econ Hist*, Supplement VI (1946), 28–49.

Herold Livesay,

1 EVANS, H. O. *Iron Pioneer, Henry W. Oliver, 1840–1904.* New York, 1942.

2 FLYNN, J. T. *God's Gold: The Story of Rockefeller and His Times.* New York, 1932.

3 GARRATY, J. A. *Right-hand Man: The Life of George W. Perkins.* New ✓ York, 1960.

4 GOODSTEIN, A. S. *Biography of a Businessman. Henry W. Sage, 1814–1897.* Ithaca, N.Y., 1962.

5 HENDRICK, B. J. *The Life of Andrew Carnegie.* 2 vols. Garden City, N.Y., ✓ 1932.

6 HUTCHINSON, W. T. *Cyrus Hall McCormick.* 2 vols. New York and London, 1930–1935.

7 JENKINS, J. W. *James B. Duke, Master Builder.* New York, 1927.

8 JOSEPHSON, Matthew. *Edison.* New York, 1959.†

9 LOTH, David. *Swope of G. E.: The Story of Gerard Swope and General Electric in American Business.* New York, 1958.

10 Mac DONALD, Forrest. *Insull.* Chicago, 1962.

11 MILLER, William. "American Historians and the Business Elite." *J Econ Hist*, IX (1949), 184–208.

12 MYERS, Gustavus. *History of the Great American Fortunes.* 3 vols. Chicago, 1909–1910.

13 NEVINS, Allan. *Study in Power: John D. Rockefeller, Industralist and Philanthropist.* 2 vols. New York, 1953.

14 NEVINS, Allan, and F. E. HILL. *Ford.* 3 vols. New York, 1954–1963.

15 PORTER, K. W. "Trends in American Business Biography." *J Econ Bus Hist*, IV (1931–1932), 583–610.

16 PROUT, H. G. *A Life of George Westinghouse.* New York, 1921.

17 REDLICH, Fritz. "The Business Leader as a 'Daimonic' Figure." *Am J Econ Socio*, XII (1953), 163–178, 289–299.

18 ROBERTS, S. I. "Portrait of a Robber Baron: Charles T. Yerkes." *Bus Hist Rev*, XXXV (1961), 344–371.

19 ROCKEFELLER, J. D. *Random Reminiscences of Men and Events.* Garden City, N.Y., 1933.

20 SCHLEGEL, M. W. *Ruler of the Reading: The Life of Franklin B. Gowen, 1836–1889.* Harrisburg, Pa., 1947.

21 STEIGERWALT, A. K. *The National Association of Manufacturers, 1895–1914: A Study in Business Leadership.* Ann Arbor, Mich., 1964.

22 SWARD, K. T. *The Legend of Henry Ford.* New York, 1948.†

23 SWIFT, L. F. *The Yankee of the Yards—the Biography of Gustavus Franklin Swift.* New York, 1927.

✓ 24 TARBELL, I. M. *The Life of Elbert H. Gary. The Story of Steel.* New York and London, 1925.

25 TAUSSIG, F. W., and C. S. JOSLYN. *American Business Leaders: A Study in Social Origins and Social Stratification.* New York, 1932.

1 TIPPLE, John. "The Anatomy of Prejudice: Origins of the Robber Baron Legend." *Bus Hist Rev*, XXXIII (1959), 510–522.

2 WALL, J. F. *Andrew Carnegie.* New York, 1970.

E. Business Organization: Corporations, Competition, Consolidations

3 ADELMAN, M. A. "The Measurement of Industrial Combination." *Rev Econ Stat*, XXXIII (1951), 269–296.

4 BERGLUND, Abraham. *The United States Steel Corporation. A Study of the Growth and Influence of Combination in the Iron and Steel Industry.* New York, 1907.

5 BRIDGE, J. H. *The Inside Story of the Carnegie Steel Company: A Romance of Millions.* New York, 1903.

6 CHANDLER, A. D., Jr. "The Beginnings of 'Big Business' in American History." *Bus Hist Rev*, XXXIII (1959), 2–31.

7 CHANDLER, A. D., Jr. *Strategy and Structure: Chapters in the History of the Industrial Enterprise.* Cambridge, Mass., 1962.†

8 DANIELIAN, N. R. *A. T. & T., The Story of Industrial Conquest.* New York, 1939.

9 EICHNER, A. S. *The Emergence of Oligopoly: Sugar Refining as a Case Study.* Baltimore, 1969.

10 EVANS, G. H., Jr. *Business Incorporations in the United States, 1800–1943.* New York, 1948.

11 HAWKINS, D. F. "The Development of Modern Financial Reporting Practices Among American Manufacturing Corporations." *Bus Hist Rev*, XXXVII (1963), 135–168.

12 HURST, J. W. *The Legitimacy of the Business Corporation in the Law of the United States, 1780–1970.* Charlottesville, Va., 1970.

13 MUSSEY, H. R. *Combination of the Mining Industry: A Study of Concentration in Lake Superior Iron Ore Production.* New York, 1905.

14 NELSON, Ralph L. *Merger Movements in American Industry, 1895–1956.* Princeton, 1959.

15 STEHMAN, J. W. *The Financial History of the American Telephone and Telegraph Company.* Boston and New York, 1925.

16 STIGLER, G. J. *Five Lectures on Economic Problems.* New York, 1950.

17 United States, Industrial Commission. *Report on Trusts and Industrial Combinations.* Vols. I, XIII. Washington, D.C., 1900, 1901.

18 WARNER, W. L. *The Corporation in the Emergent American Society.* New York, 1962.

19 YEARLEY, C. K., Jr. *Enterprise and Anthracite. Economics and Democracy in Schuylkill County, 1820–1875.* Baltimore, 1961.

F. The Regulation of Enterprise

1. GENERAL WORKS AND THEORY

1 BLUM, J. M. *The Republican Roosevelt.* Cambridge, Mass., 1954.†

2 BRANDEIS, L. D. *The Curse of Bigness: Miscellaneous Papers.* New York, 1934.

3 DESTLER, C. M. "The Opposition of American Businessmen to Social Control During the 'Gilded Age.'" *Miss Val Hist Rev,* XXXIX (1953), 641–672.

4 DIAMOND, William. *The Economic Thought of Woodrow Wilson.* Baltimore, 1943.

5 FAIRMAN, Charles. *Mr. Justice Miller and the Supreme Court 1862–1890.* Cambridge, Mass., 1939.

6 HACKER, L. M. *The Triumph of American Capitalism: The Development of Forces in American History to the End of the Nineteenth Century.* New York, 1947.

7 HOFSTADTER, Richard. *The Age of Reform: From Bryan to F.D.R.* New York, 1955.†

8 HUTHMACHER, J. J. "Urban Liberalism and the Age of Reform." *Miss Val Hist Rev,* XLIX (1962), 231–241.

9 JACOBS, C. E. *Law Writers and the Courts. The Influence of Thomas M. Cooley, Christopher G. Tiedeman, and John F. Dillon upon American Constitutional Law.* Berkeley and Los Angeles, 1954.

10 JONES, Alan. "Thomas M. Cooley and 'Laissez-Faire Constitutionalism': A Reconsideration." *J Am Hist,* LIII (1967), 751–771.

11 JONES, Alan. "Thomas M. Cooley and the Interstate Commerce Commission: Continuity and Change in the Doctrine of Equal Rights." *Pol Sci Q,* LXXXI (1966), 602–627.

12 KOLKO, Gabriel. *The Triumph of Conservatism. A Reinterpretation of American History, 1900–1916.* New York, 1963.†

13 LEVINE, Daniel. *Varieties of Reform Thought.* Madison, Wis., 1964.

14 LINK, A. S. *Wilson: The New Freedom.* Princeton, 1956.†

15 Mc CLOSKEY, R. G. *American Conservatism in the Age of Enterprise. A Study of William Graham Sumner, Stephen J. Field, and Andrew Carnegie.* Cambridge, Mass., 1951.†

16 MAGRATH, C. P. *Morrison R. Waite; The Triumph of Character.* New York, 1963.

17 MOWRY, G. E. *The Era of Theodore Roosevelt, 1900–1912.* New York, 1958.†

1 PAUL, A. M. *Conservative Crisis and the Rule of Law: Attitudes of Bar and Bench. 1887–1895.* Ithaca, N.Y., 1960.†

2 SWISHER, C. B. *Stephen J. Field, Craftsman of the Law.* Washington, D.C., 1930.

3 TWISS, B. R. *Lawyers and the Constitution. How Laissez Faire Came to the Supreme Court.* Princeton, 1942.

4 WIEBE, R. H. *Businessmen and Reform: A Study of the Progressive Movement.* Cambridge, Mass., 1962.†

5 WIEBE, R. H. *The Search for Order, 1877–1920.* New York, 1967.†

6 WILSON, Woodrow. *The New Freedom.* New York and Garden City, N.Y., 1913.†

2. REGULATION OF RAILROADS: STATE AND NATION

7 BENSON, Lee. *Merchants, Farmers and Railroads: Railroad Regulation and New York Politics, 1850–1887.* Cambridge, Mass., 1955.

8 BLACKFORD, M. G. "Business Men and the Regulation of Railroads and Public Utilities in California During the Progressive Era." *Bus Hist Rev,* XLIV (1970), 307–319.

9 BLUM, J. M. "Theodore Roosevelt and the Hepburn Act." *The Letters of Theodore Roosevelt.* Ed. by E. E. Morrison. Vol. VI. Cambridge, Mass., 1952, pp. 1558–1571.

10 CAINE, S. P. *The Myth of a Progressive Reform: Railroad Regulation in Wisconsin, 1903–1910.* Madison, Wis., 1970.

11 COTNER, Robert C. *James Stephen Hogg, A Biography.* Austin, 1959.

12 DECKER, L. E. *Railroads, Lands, and Politics: The Taxation of the Railroad Land Grants, 1864–1897.* Providence, 1964.

13 DOSTER, J. F. *Railroads in Alabama Politics, 1875–1914.* University, Ala., 1957.

14 HUNT, R. S. *Law and Locomotives. The Impact of the Railroad on Wisconsin Law in the Nineteenth Century.* Madison, Wis., 1958.

15 KOLKO, Gabriel. *Railroads and Regulation, 1877–1916.* Princeton, 1965.

16 MAC AVOY, Paul W. *The Economic Effects of Regulation. The Trunk-line Railroad Cartels and the Interstate Commission Before 1900.* Cambridge, Mass., 1965.

17 MILLER, G. H. "Origins of the Iowa Granger Law." *Miss Val Hist Rev,* XL (1954), 657–680.

18 NASH, G. D. "Origins of the Interstate Commerce Act of 1887." *Penn Hist,* XXIV (1957), 181–190.

19 NASH, G. D. "The Reformer Reformed: John H. Reagan and Railroad Regulation." *Bus Hist Rev,* XXIX (1955), 189–196.

1 PURCELL, E. A., Jr. "Ideas and Interests: Business and the Interstate Commerce Act." *J Am Hist*, LIV (1967), 561–578.

2 RIPLEY, W. Z. *Railroads: Rates and Regulation.* New York, 1912.

3 United States Congress, Senate. *Report of the Select Committee on Transportation Routes to the Seaboard* (Windom Report). 43d Cong. 1st sess., Sen. Rep. No. 307, Pts. 1–2 (1874).

4 United States Congress, Senate. *Report of the Senate Select Committee on Interstate Commerce* (Cullom Report). 49th Cong. 1st sess., Sen. Rep. No. 46, Pts. 1–2 (1886).

3. THE ANTITRUST MOVEMENT

5 HANDLER, Milton. *Antitrust in Perspective: the Complementary Roles of Rule and Discretion.* New York, 1957.

6 HANDLER, Milton. *A Study of the Construction and Enforcement of the Federal Antitrust Laws.* Monograph 38. Temporary National Economic Committee (TNEC). Washington, D.C., 1941.

7 JENKS, J. W., and W. E. CLARK. *The Trust Problem.* Garden City, N.Y., 1929.

8 JOHNSON, A. M. "Antitrust Policy in Transition, 1908: Ideal and Reality." *Miss Val Hist Rev*, XLVIII (1961), 415–434.

9 LETWIN, William. *Law and Economic Policy in America: The Evolution of the Sherman Antitrust Act.* New York, 1965.

10 NEALE, A. D. *The Antitrust Laws of the United States of America. A Study of Competition Enforced by Law.* Cambridge, Eng., 1960.

11 RIPLEY, W. Z. *Main Street and Wall Street.* Boston, 1927.

12 TAFT, W. H. *The Anti-Trust Act and the Supreme Court.* New York and London, 1914.

13 THORELLI, H. B. *The Federal Antitrust Policy. Origination of an American Tradition.* Baltimore, 1955.

G. Labor

1. GENERAL WORKS

14 DOUGLAS, P. H. *American Apprenticeship and Industrial Education.* New York, 1921.

15 LEVASSEUR, E. *The American Workman.* Baltimore, 1900.

16 United States, Commission on Industrial Relations. *Final Report and Testimony by the Commission on Industrial Relations . . . 1912.* 64th Cong. 1st sess. Senate Documents, 415. 11 vols. Washington, D.C., 1916.

1 United States, Industrial Commission. *Report . . . on the Relations and Conditions of Capital and Labor . . . in Manufactures and General Business.* Vols. VII and XIV. Washington, D.C., 1901.

2. *CONSTITUENTS OF THE LABOR FORCE*

2 BANCROFT, Gertrude. *The American Labor Force. Its Growth and Changing Composition.* New York, 1958.

3 BERTHOFF, R. T. *British Immigrants in Industrial America, 1790–1950.* Cambridge, Mass., 1953.

4 DUBOFSKY, Melvyn. "Organized Labor and the Immigrant in New York City, 1900–1918." *Labor History,* II (1961), 182–201.

5 DURAND, John D. *The Labor Force in the United States, 1890–1960.* New York, 1948.

6 ERICKSON, Charlotte. *American Industry and the European Immigrant, 1860–1885.* Cambridge, Mass., 1957.

7 FOERSTER, R. F. *The Italian Emigration of Our Times.* Cambridge, Mass., 1919.

8 GOODRICH, Carter, and Sol DAVISON. "The Wage Earner in the Westward Movement." *Pol Sci Q,* L (1935), 161–185; LI (1936), 61–116.

9 GROB, G. N. "Organized Labor and the Negro Worker, 1865–1900." *Labor History,* I (1960), 164–176.

10 HANDLIN, Oscar. "International Migration and the Acquisition of New Skills." *The Progress of Underdeveloped Areas.* Ed. by B. E. Hoselitz. Chicago, 1952.

11 HEALD, Morrell. "Business Attitudes Toward European Immigration." *J Econ Hist,* XIII (1953), 291–304.

12 HILL, Joseph A. *Women in Gainful Occupations, 1870 to 1920.* Census (1920) Monographs. Washington, D.C., 1929.

13 JEROME, Harry. *Migration and Business Cycles.* New York, 1926.

14 JONES, M. A. *American Immigration.* Chicago, 1960.†

15 KENNEDY, L. V. *The Negro Peasant Turns Cityward. Effects of Recent Migrations to Northern Centers.* New York, 1930.

16 KUZNETS, Simon, and Dorothy S. THOMAS, eds. *Population Redistribution and Economic Growth, United States, 1870–1950.* 3 vols. Philadelphia, 1957–1964.

17 LEBERGOTT, Stanley. *Manpower in Economic Growth. The American Record Since 1800.* See 3.10.

18 MILLER, A. R. "Components of Labor Force Growth." *J Econ Hist,* XXII (1962), 47–58.

19 THOMAS, Brinley. *Migration and Economic Growth.* Cambridge, Eng., 1954.

1 United States, Immigration Commission. *Reports*. Vol. I–II, "Abstract of Reports"; Vol. III, "Statistical Review of Immigration, 1820–1910"; Vols. VI–XXV, Pts. 1–25, "Immigrants in Industries"; Vol. XXXIX, "Immigration Legislation." Washington, D.C., 1911.

2 United States Senate. *Report on Condition of Women and Child Wage-earners in the United States*. Vol. IX: "History of Women in Industry in the United States." 61st Cong. 2d. sess. Senate Doc. No 645. Washington, D.C., 1910.

3 WOODSON, C. G. *A Century of Negro Migration*. Washington, D.C., 1918.

4 YEARLEY, C. K. Jr. *Britons in American Labor: A History of the Influence of the United Kingdom Immigrants on American Labor, 1820–1914*. Baltimore, 1957.

3. LABOR CONDITIONS

5 ABBOTT, Edith. "The Wages of Unskilled Labor in the United States 1850–1900." *J Pol Econ*, XIII (1905), 321–347.

6 BRISSENDEN, P. F. *Earnings of Factory Workers, 1899 to 1927*. Census (1920) Monographs, X. Washington, D.C., 1929.

7 BUTTRICK, J. "The Inside Contract System." *J Econ Hist*, XII (1952), 205–221.

8 CAHILL, M. C. *Shorter Hours, A Study of the Movement Since the Civil War*. New York, 1932.

9 COOMBS, Whitney. *The Wages of Unskilled Labor in Manufacturing Industries in the United States, 1890–1924*. New York, 1926.

10 DOUGLAS, P. H. *Real Wages in the United States, 1890–1926*. Boston, 1930.

11 HANSEN, A. H. "Factors Affecting the Trend of Real Wages." *Am Econ Rev*, XV (1925), 27–42.

12 KUCZYNSKI, Jürgen. *A Short History of Labour Conditions Under Industrialism*. Vol. II: "The United States of America 1789 to the Present Day." London, 1944.

13 LESCOHIER, D. D. "Working Conditions." Vol. III of *History of Labor in the United States, 1896–1932*, by J. R. Commons et al. New York, 1935.

14 LONG, C. D. *Wages and Earnings in the United States, 1860–1890*. Princeton, 1960.

15 REES, Albert. *Real Wages in Manufacturing 1890–1914*. Princeton, 1961.

4. LABOR ORGANIZATIONS AND THEIR "BATTLES"

16 ANDREWS, J. B. "Nationalisation, 1860–1877." Vol. II of *History of Labour in the United States*, by J. R. Commons et al. New York, 1918.

1 BEDFORD, Henry F. *Socialism and the Workers in Massachusetts, 1886–1912.* Amherst, 1966.

2 BRISSENDEN, P. F. *The I.W.W.: A Study of American Syndicalism.* New York, 1919.

3 BRUCE, R. V. *1877: Year of Violence.* Indianapolis, 1959.

4 BUCHANAN, J. R. *The Story of a Labor Agitator.* New York, 1903.

5 BURBANK, D. T. *Reign of the Rabble. The St. Louis General Strike of 1877.* New York, 1966.

6 CONLIN, J. R. *Bread and Roses Too. Studies of the Wobblies.* Westport, Conn., 1969.

7 CORNELL, R. J. *The Anthracite Coal Strike of 1902.* Washington, D.C., 1957.

8 DAVID, Henry. *The History of the Haymarket Affair. A Study in the American Social-Revolutionary and Labor Movements.* New York, 1936.

9 DUBOFSKY, M. *We Shall Be All: A History of the Industrial Workers of the World.* Chicago, 1969.

10 DUBOFSKY, M. *When Workers Organize. New York City in the Progressive Era.* Amherst, 1968.

11 FITCH, J. A. *The Steel Workers.* New York, 1910.

12 GINGER, Ray. *The Bending Cross: a Biography of Eugene Victor Debs.* New Brunswick, N.J., 1949.†

13 GLUCK, Elsie. *John Mitchell Miner, Labor's Bargain with the Gilded Age.* New York, 1929.

14 GOLDMAN, Emma. *Living My Life.* 2 vols. New York, 1931.

15 GOMPERS, Samuel. *Seventy Years of Life and Labor: An Autobiography.* 2 vols. New York, 1925.

16 GREENE, V. R. *The Slavic Community on Strike: Immigrant Labor in Pennsylvania Anthracite.* Notre Dame, Ind., 1968.

17 GROB, G. N. *Workers and Utopia. A Study of Ideological Conflict in the American Labor Movement 1865–1900.†* See 8.3.

18 GROSSMAN, J. P. *William Sylvis, Pioneer of American Labor; A Study of the Movement During the Civil War.* New York, 1945.

19 GULICK, C. A., and M. K. BERS. "Insight and Illusion in Perlman's Theory of the Labor Movement." *Indus Labor Rel Rev,* VI (1953), 510–531.

20 HALL, J. P. "The Knights of St. Crispin in Massachusetts, 1869–1878." *J Econ Hist,* XVIII (1958), 161–175.

21 HARRIS, Herbert. *American Labor.* New Haven, Conn., 1939.

22 HARVEY, K. A. *The Best-Dressed Miners. Life and Labor in the Maryland Coal Region, 1835–1910.* Ithaca, N.Y., and London, 1969.

1 HARVEY, R. H. *Samuel Gompers, Champion of the Toiling Masses.* Stanford, 1935.

2 HINRICHS, A. F. *The United Mine Workers of America and the Non-Union Coal Fields.* New York, 1923.

3 HOAGLAND, H. E. "The Rise of the Iron Moulders' International Union." *Am Econ Rev,* III (1913), 296–313.

4 HUNT, E. E., F. H. TRYON, and J. H. WILLITS, eds. *What the Coal Commission Found, An Authoritative Summary.* Baltimore, 1925.

5 LANE, W. D. *Civil War in West Virginia: A Story of the Industrial Conflict in the Coal Mines.* New York, 1921.

6 LASLETT, John. "Reflections on the Failure of Socialism in the American Federation of Labor." *Miss Val Hist Rev,* L (1964), 634–651.

7 LESCOHIER, D. D. *The Knights of St. Crispin, 1867–1874: A Study in the Industrial Causes of Trade Unionism.* Madison, Wis., 1910.

8 LEVINE, Louis. *The Women's Garment Workers.* New York, 1924.

9 LINDSEY, Almont. *The Pullman Strike.* Chicago, 1942.†

10 LORWIN, L. L. *The American Federation of Labor: History, Policies, and Prospects.* Washington, D.C., 1933.

11 Mc MURRY, D. L. *The Great Burlington Strike of 1888. A Case History in Labor Relations.* Cambridge, Mass., 1956.

12 Mc NEILL, G. E. *The Labor Movement: The Problem of To-day.* New York, 1891.

13 PERLMAN, Selig. "Upheaval and Reorganization (Since 1876)." Vol. II of *History of Labour in the United States,* by J. R Commons et al. New York, 1918.

14 PERLMAN, Selig, and Philip TAFT. "Labor Movements." Vol. IV of *History of Labor in the United States,* by J. R. Commons et al. New York, 1935.

15 POWDERLY, T. V. *The Path I Trod.* New York, 1940.

16 POWDERLY, T. V. *Thirty Years of Labor, 1859 to 1889.* Philadelphia, 1890.

17 REED, L. S. *The Labor Philosophy of Samuel Gompers.* New York, 1930.

18 RENSHAW, Patrick. *The Wobblies. The Story of Syndicalism in the United States.* Garden City, N.Y., 1967.†

19 SHANNON, D. A. *The Socialist Party of America.* New York, 1955.†

20 STALEY, Eugene. *History of the Illinois State Federation of Labor.* Chicago, 1930.

21 SUFFERN, A, E. *The Coal Miner's Struggle for Industrial Status.* Washington, D.C., 1926.

1   TAFT, Philip. *The A. F. of L. from the Death of Gompers to the Merger.* New York, 1959.

2   TAFT, Philip. *The A. F. of L. in the Time of Gompers.* New York, 1957.

3   TAFT, Philip. *Organized Labor in American History.* New York, 1964.

4   ULMAN, Lloyd. *The Rise of the National Trade Union.* Cambridge, Mass., 1955.

5   United States, Anthracite Coal Strike Commission. *Report to the President on the Anthracite Coal Strike of May–October, 1902.* Washington, D.C., 1903.

6   United States, Bureau of Labor. *Report on the Strike of Textile Workers in Lawrence, Mass., in 1912.* 62d Cong., 2nd sess., Sen. Doc. No. 870. Washington, D.C., 1912.

7   United States, Congress, House. *House Reports* No. 2447 (Homestead Strike). 52d Cong., 2nd sess. Washington, D.C., 1893.

8   United States, Congress, Senate. *Senate Reports* No. 1280 (Homestead Strike). 52d Cong., 2nd sess. Washington, D.C., 1893.

9   United States, Congress, Senate. *Report on Condition of Women and Child Wage-Earners in the United States.* Vol. X: "History of Women in Trade Unions." 61st Cong., 2d sess., Sen. Doc. No. 645. Washington, D.C., 1911.

10   WARE, N. J. *The Labor Movement in the United States, 1860–1895.* New York, 1929.†

11   WIEBE, R. H. "The Anthracite Strike of 1902: A Record of Confusion." *Miss Val Hist Rev*, XLVIII (1961), 229–251.

12   WOLMAN, Leo. *The Growth of American Trade Unions, 1880–1923.* New York, 1924.

13   WRIGHT, C. D. "The Amalgamated Association of Iron and Steel Workers." *Q J Econ*, VII (1893), 400–432.

14   WRIGHT, C. D. *The Battles of Labor.* Philadelphia, 1906.

15   YELLEN, Samuel. *American Labor Struggles.* New York, 1936.

5. EMPLOYERS' LABOR POLICY

16   AITKEN, H. G. J. *Taylorism at Watertown Arsenal. Scientific Management in Action, 1908–1915.* See 19.17.

17   BONNETT, C. E. *History of Employers' Associations in the United States.* New York, 1956.

18   BRODY, David. *Steelworkers in America: The Nonunion Era.* Cambridge, Mass., 1960.

19   BROEHL, W. G. *The Molly Maguires.* Cambridge, Mass., 1964.

20   BUDER, Stanley. *Pullman: An Experiment in Industrial Order and Community Planning, 1880–1930.* New York, 1967.

ERA OF RAPID ECONOMIC GROWTH, 1877–1914 **33**

1 COLEMAN, J. W. *The Molly Maguire Riots, Industrial Conflict in the Pennsylvania Coal Region.* Richmond, Va., 1936.

2 GARRATY, J. A. "The United States Steel Corporation Versus Labor: The Early Years." *Labor History,* I (1960), 3–38.

3 GULICK, C. A., Jr. *Labor Policy of the United States Steel Corporation.* New York, 1924.

4 HERRING, H. L. *Welfare Work in Mill Villages: The Story of Extra-Mill Activities in North Carolina.* Chapel Hill, N.C., 1929.

5 Mc MURRY, D. L. "Labor Policies of the General Managers' Association of Chicago, 1886–1894." *J Econ Hist,* XIII (1953), 160–178.

6 OZANNE, Robert. *A Century of Labor-Management Relations at McCormick and International Harvester.* Madison, Wis., 1967.

7 SCHLEGEL, M. W. *Ruler of the Reading: The Life of Franklin B. Gowen, 1836–1889.* Harrisburg, Pa., 1947.

8 TAYLOR, A. G. *Labor Policies of the National Association of Manufacturers.* Urbana, Ill., 1928.

9 United States, Congress, Senate. *Report on Conditions of Employment in the Iron and Steel Industry in the United States.* Senate Reports No. 110. 4 vols. 62d Cong., 1st sess. Washington, D.C., 1913.

10 United States, Industrial Commission. *Report on . . . Capital and Labor . . . in the Mining Industry.* Vol. XII. Washington, D.C., 1901.

11 WILLOUGHBY, W. F. "Employer's Associations for Dealing with Labor in the United States." *Q J Econ,* XX (1905), 110–150.

12 WOOD, N. J. "Industrial Relations Policies of American Management, 1900–1933." *Bus Hist Rev,* XXXIV (1960), 403–420.

6. LABOR AND THE GOVERNMENT

13 ADAMS, Graham. *Age of Industrial Violence 1910–1915: The Activities and Findings of the United States Commission on Industrial Relations.* New York, 1966.

14 AUERBACH, J. S. "Progressives at Sea: The La Follette Act of 1915." *Labor History,* II (1961), 344–360.

15 BAKER, E. F. *Protective Labor Legislation with Special Reference to Women in the State of New York.* New York, 1925.

16 BARNARD, J. L. *Factory Legislation in Pennsylvania, Its History and Administration.* Philadelphia, 1907.

17 BECKNER, E. R. *A History of Labor Legislation in Illinois.* Chicago, 1929.

18 BERMAN, Edward. *Labor and the Sherman Act.* New York and London, 1930.

19 BERMAN, Edward. *Labor Disputes and the President of the United States.* New York, 1924.

1 BRANDEIS, Elizabeth. "Labor Legislation." Vol. III of *History of Labor in the United States, 1896–1932*, by J. R. Commons et al. New York, 1935.

2 CARROLL, M. R. *Labor and Politics: The Attitude of the American Federation of Labor Toward Legislation and Politics.* Boston and New York, 1923.

3 EDWARDS, A. M. *The Labor Legislation of Connecticut.* New York, 1907.

4 EGGERT, G. G. *Railroad Labor Disputes: The Beginnings of Federal Strike Policy.* Ann Arbor, Mich., 1967.

5 FAIRCHILD, F. R. *The Factory Legislation of the State of New York.* New York, 1906.

6 FIELD, A. S. *The Child Labor Policy of New Jersey.* Cambridge, Mass., 1909.

7 FRANKFURTER, Felix, and Nathan GREENE. *The Labor Injunction.* New York, 1930.

8 GOLDMARK, J. C. *Impatient Crusader: Florence Kelley's Life Story.* Urbana, Ill., 1953.

9 GREGORY, C. O. *Labor and the Law.* New York, 1961.

10 GROAT, G. G. *Attitude of American Courts on Labor Cases.* New York, 1911.

11 LEIBY, James. *Carroll Wright and Labor Reform. The Origin of Labor Statistics.* Cambridge, Mass., 1960.

12 LIEF, Alfred, ed. *The Dissenting Opinions of Mr. Justice Holmes.* New York, 1929.

13 LIEF, Alfred, ed. *The Social and Economic Views of Mr. Justice Brandeis.* New York, 1930.

14 MASON, A. T. *Organized Labor and the Law, with Special Reference to the Sherman and Clayton Acts.* Durham, N.C., 1925.

15 PERSONS, C. E., et al. *Labor Laws and Their Enforcement with Special Reference to Massachusetts.* New York, 1911.

16 TOWLES, J. K. *Factory Legislation of Rhode Island.* Princeton, 1908.

17 United States, Congress, Senate. *Report on Condition of Women and Child Wage-Earners in the United States.* Senate Document No. 645. Vol. VI: "The Beginnings of Child Labor Legislation in Certain States." 61st Cong., 2d sess. Washington, D.C., 1910.

18 United States, Congress, Senate. *Report on Condition of Women and Child Wage-Earners in the United States.* Senate Document No. 645. Vol. XIX: "Labor Laws and Factory Conditions." 61st Cong., 2d sess. Washington, D.C., 1912.

19 United States, Industrial Commission. *Reports . . . on Labor Organizations, Labor Disputes, and Arbitration, and on Railway Labor.* Vol. XVII. Washington, D.C., 1901.

1 United States, Strike Commission. *Report on the Chicago Strike of June–July, 1894.* Washington, D.C., 1895.

2 WITTE, E. E. *The Government in Labor Disputes.* New York and London, 1932.

H.   Domestic Markets and Distribution

3 ATHERTON, L. E. *Main Street on the Middle Border.* Bloomington, Ind., 1954, pp. 43–57.†

4 BARGER, H. *Distribution's Place in the American Economy Since 1869.* Princeton, 1955.

5 BULLOCK, R. J. "The Early History of the Great Atlantic and Pacific Tea Company." *Har Bus Rev*, XI (1933), 289–298.

6 BULLOCK, R. J. "A History of the Great Atlantic and Pacific Tea Company Since 1878." *Har Bus Rev*, XII (1933), 59–69.

7 CLARK, T. D. *Pills, Petticoats and Plows.* Indianapolis, 1944.

8 EMMET, B., and J. E. JEUCK. *Catalogues and Counters. A History of Sears Roebuck and Company.* Chicago, 1950.

9 GIBBONS, H. A. *John Wanamaker.* New York, 1926.

10 HOWER, R. M. *History of Macy's of New York, 1858–1919.* Cambridge, Mass., 1943.

11 HOWER, R. M. *The History of an Advertising Agency: N. W. Ayer and Son at Work, 1869–1939.* Cambridge, Mass., 1949.

12 NYSTROM, P. H. *The Economics of Retailing.* 2 vols., 3d ed. New York, 1930.

13 PRESBREY, F. *The History and Development of Advertising.* New York, 1929.

14 RESSEGUIE, H. E. "Alexander Turney Stewart and the Development of the Department Store, 1823–1876." *Bus Hist Rev*, XXXIX (1965), 301-322.

15 TWYMAN, D. W. *History of Marshall Field & Co., 1852–1906.* Philadelphia, 1954.

16 United States, Industrial Commission. Vol. XIX. Washington, D.C., 1902, pp. 544–549.

17 WENDT, L., and H. KOGAN. *Give the Lady What She Wants.* Chicago, 1952.†

18 WINKLER, J. K. *Five and Ten: The Fabulous Life of F. W. Woolworth.* New York, 1940.

19 WOOD, J. P. *The Story of Advertising.* New York, 1958.

I.   Finance and Banking

20 ADLER, Cyrus. *Jacob H. Schiff. His Life and Letters.* 2 vols. Garden City, N.Y., 1929.

1 ALLEN, F. L. *The Great Pierpont Morgan.* New York, 1949.†

2 BARNES, J. A. *John G. Carlisle, Financial Statesman.* New York, 1931.

3 BARNETT, G. E. *State Banks and Trust Companies Since the Passage of the National-Bank Act.* Washington, D.C., 1911.

4 BRANDEIS, L. D. *Other People's Money and How the Bankers Use It.* New York, 1914.†

5 BULEY, C. R. *The Equitable Life Assurance Society of the United States.* New York, 1959.

6 CAROSSO, V. P. *Investment Banking in America: A History.* Cambridge, Mass., 1970.

7 CHANDLER, A. D. *Henry Varnum Poor—Business Editor, Analyst and Reformer.* Cambridge, Mass., 1956.

8 CLEWS, Henry. *Fifty Years in Wall Street.* New York, 1908.

9 CLOUGH, S. B. *A Century of American Life Insurance: A History of the Mutual Life Insurance Company of New York, 1843–1943.* New York, 1946.

10 DAVIS, L. E. "The Investment Market, 1870–1914: The Evolution of a National Market." *J Econ Hist,* XXV (1965), 355–399.

11 FRIEDMAN, Milton, and A. J. SCHWARTZ. *A Monetary History of the United States, 1867–1960.*† See 2.19.

12 GLASS, Carter. *An Adventure in Constructive Finance.* New York, 1927.

13 GOODHART, C. A. E. *The New York Money Market and the Finance of Trade, 1900–1913.* Cambridge, Mass., 1969.

14 HARVEY, W. H. *Coin's Financial School.* Ed. by Richard Hofstadter. Cambridge, Mass., 1963.†

15 HICKS, J. D. *The Populist Revolt.*† See 10.6.

16 HOYT, E. P. *The House of Morgan.* New York, 1966.

17 JAMES, F. C. *The Growth of Chicago Banks.* 2 vols. New York and London, 1938.

18 KINLEY, David. *The Independent Treasury of the United States and Its Relations to the Banks of the Country.* Washington, D.C., 1911.

19 KOLKO, Gabriel. *The Triumph of Conservatism. A Reinterpretation of American History, 1900–1916.* New York, 1963, pp. 317–354.†

20 KROOSS, H. E., and P. STUDENSKI. *Financial History of the United States; Fiscal, Monetary, Banking and Tariff, Including Financial Administration and State and Local Finance.* New York, 1963.

21 LARSON, H. M. *Jay Cooke, Private Banker.* Cambridge, Mass., 1936.

22 LAUGHLIN, J. L. *The Federal Reserve Act: Its Origin and Problems.* New York, 1933.

1 LAWSON, T. W. *Frenzied Finance.* New York, 1905.

2 LINK, A. S. *Wilson: The New Freedom.* Princeton, 1956, pp. 199–240.†

3 McELROY, Robert M. *Levi Parsons Morton, Banker, Diplomat, Statesman.* New York and London, 1930.

4 MOODY, John. *The Long Road Home.* New York, 1934.

5 MYERS, M. G. *The New York Money Market, Origins and Development.* New York, 1931–1932.

6 NAVIN, T. R., and M. V. SEARS. "The Rise of the Market for Industrial Securities, 1887–1902." *Bus Hist Rev,* XIX (1955), 105–138.

7 NORTH, D. C. "Life Insurance and Investment Banking at the Time of the Armstrong Investigation of 1905–1906." *J Econ Hist,* XIV (1954), 209–228.

8 NOYES, A. D. *Forty Years of American Finance: A Short Financial History of the Government and People of the United States Since the Civil War, 1865–1907.* New York and London, 1909.

9 REDLICH, Fritz. *The Molding of American Banking; Men and Ideas.* Vol. II, Pt. 2: *1840–1910.* New York, 1951.

10 SPRAGUE, O. M. W. *History of Crises Under the National Banking System.* Washington, D.C., 1910.

11 TAUS, E. R. *Central Banking Functions of the United States Treasury, 1789–1941.* New York, 1943.

12 TRESCOTT, P. B. *Financing American Enterprise: The Story of Commercial Banking.* New York, 1963.

13 UNGER, Irwin. *The Greenback Era: A Social and Political History of American Finance.* Princeton, 1964.†

14 United States, Congress, House. *Report of a Subcommittee of the Committee on Currency and Banking Appointed to Investigate the Concentration of Control of Money and Credit* (Pujo Committee). Government Documents, Serial Number 6340. Washington, D.C., 1913.

15 WARBURG, P. M. *The Federal Reserve System: Its Origin and Growth.* 2 vols. New York, 1930.

16 WEINSTEIN, Allen. "Was There a 'Crime of 1873?'; The Case of the Demonitized Dollar." *J Am Hist,* LIV (1967), 307–326.

17 WILLIAMSON, H. F. *Northwestern Mutual Life: A Century of Trusteeship.* Evanston, Ill., 1957.

18 WILLIS, H. P. *The Federal Reserve System, Legislation, Organization, and Operation.* New York, 1923.

J. *International Trade and Investment*

1. *GENERAL WORKS*

19 BULLOCK, C. J., J. H. WILLIAMS, and R. S. TUCKER. "The Balance of Trade of the United States." *Rev Econ Stat,* I (1919), 215–266.

1 CROLY, H. D. *Willard Straight*. New York, 1924.

2 FIELD, J. A., Jr. *America and the Mediterranean World, 1776–1882.* Princeton, 1969.

3 GRISWOLD, A. W. *The Far Eastern Policy of the United States.* New York, 1938.†

4 KEENLEYSIDE, H. L. *Canada and the United States.* New York, 1952.

5 LaFEBER, W. *The New Empire. An Interpretation of American Expansion, 1860–1898.* Ithaca, N.Y., 1963.†

6 PRATT, Julius. *Expansionists of 1898.* Baltimore, 1936.†

7 REYES, J. S. *Legislative History of America's Economic Policy Toward the Philippines.* New York, 1923.

8 SCHMECKEBIER, L. F., and G. A. WEBER. *The Bureau of Foreign and Domestic Commerce: Its History, Activities, and Organization.* Baltimore, 1924.

9 STEVENS, S. K. *American Expansion in Hawaii, 1842–1898.* Harrisburg, Pa., 1945.

10 TATE, Merze. *Hawaii: Reciprocity or Annexation.* East Lansing, Mich., 1968.

11 TAUSSIG, F. W. *The Tariff History of the United States.* 8th ed. New York and London, 1931.†

12 THOMAS, Brinley. *Migration and Economic Growth. A Study of Great Britain and the Atlantic Economy.* See 28.19.

13 United States, Tariff Commission. *Reciprocity and Commercial Treaties.* Washington, D.C., 1919.

14 VAN ALSTYNE, R. W. *The Rising American Empire.* Oxford and New York, 1960.†

15 WILKINS, Mira. *The Emergence of Multinational Enterprise: American Business Abroad from the Colonial Era to 1914.* Cambridge, Mass., 1970.

16 WILLIAMSON, J. G. *American Growth and the Balance of Payments, 1820–1913.* Chapel Hill, N.C., 1964.

2. COMMODITY TRADES

17 CAMPBELL, G. S., Jr. *Special Business Interests and the Open Door Policy.* New Haven, Conn., 1951.

18 DAVIES, R. B. " 'Peacefully Working to Conquer the World.' The Singer Manufacturing Company in Foreign Markets, 1854–1889." *Bus Hist Rev*, XLIII (1969), 299–325.

19 DENNETT, Tyler. *Americans in Eastern Asia. A Critical Study of the Policy of the United States ... in the 19th Century.* New York, 1922.

1 HIDY, R. W. and M. E. *History of Standard Oil Company (New Jersey). Pioneering in Big Business, 1882–1911*, pp. 122–134, 233–268, 494–579. See 22.5.

2 HUTCHINS, J. G. B. *The American Maritime Industries and Public Policy, 1789–1914*. Cambridge, Mass., 1941.

3 HUTCHINSON, W. T. *Cyrus Hall McCormick*. 2 vols. New York and London, 1930–1935.

4 JENKINS, J. W. *James B. Duke, Master Builder*. New York, 1927.

5 LIPSEY, R. E. *Price and Quantity Trends in the Foreign Trade of the United States*. See 3.11.

6 McCORMICK, T. J. *China Market: America's Quest for Informal Empire, 1893–1908*. Chicago, 1967.

7 MINTZ, Isaac. "American Exports During Business Cycles, 1879–1958." *Occasional Paper* No. 76, National Bureau of Economic Research. New York, 1961.

8 NEVINS, Allan, and F. E. HILL. *Ford: The Times, the Man, the Company. 1863–1915*. New York, 1954.

9 NEVINS, Allan, and F. E. HILL. *Ford: Expansion and Challenge. 1915–1933*. New York, 1957, pp. 355–378; 541–569.

10 NEVINS, Allan, and F. E. HILL. *Ford: Decline and Rebirth. 1933–1962*. New York, 1962, pp. 77–103; 273–293; 389–405.

11 NORTH, D. C. "Ocean Freight Rates and Economic Development 1750–1913." *J Econ Hist*, XVIII (1958), 537–555.

12 NOURSE, E. G. *American Agriculture and the European Market*. New York, 1924.

13 ROTHSTEIN, Morton. "The International Market for Agricultural Commodities, 1850–1873." *Economic Change in the Civil War Era*. Ed. by D. T. Gilchrist and W. D. Lewis. See 5.10.

14 TRIMBLE, William. "Historical Aspects of the Surplus Food Production of the United States, 1862–1902." *Ann Rep Am Hist Assn*, I (1918), 223–239.

15 United States Commissioner of Corporations. *Reports . . . on the Tobacco Industry*. Pt. 1. Washington, D.C., 1909.

16 VARG, P. A. "The Myth of the China Market, 1890–1914." *Am Hist Rev*, LXXIII (1968), 742–758.

17 WILLIAMSON, H. F., and A. R. DAUM. *The American Petroleum Industry 1859–1959*. 2 vols. Vol. I, pp. 309–340, 553–722. Vol. II, pp. 242–260. See 22.15.

3. INVESTMENT

18 ADAMS, F. U. *Conquest of the Tropics; The Story of the Creative Enterprises Conducted by the United Fruit Company*. New York, 1914.

1 CLEMENT, R. V. "The Farmers' Attitude Toward British Investment in American Industry." *J Econ Hist*, XV (1955), 151–159.

2 CLYDE, P. H. *International Rivalries in Manchuria, 1689–1922.* Columbus, Ohio, 1926.

3 CROLY, H. D. *Willard Straight.* New York, 1924.

4 CURRIE, A. W. "British Attitudes Toward Investment in North American Railroads." *Bus Hist Rev*, XXXIV (1960), 194–215.

5 ESTHUS, R. A. *Theodore Roosevelt and Japan.* Seattle, 1966, pp. 112–127, 229–245.

6 FIELD, F. V. *American Participation in the China Consortiums.* Chicago, 1931.

7 HARRINGTON, F. H. *God, Mammon, and the Japanese.* Madison, Wis., 1944.

8 HOU, Chi-Ming. *Foreign Investment and Economic Development in China, 1840–1937.* Cambridge, Mass., 1965.

9 JENKS, L. H. *The Migration of British Capital to 1875.* New York, 1927.

10 KEPNER, C. D. *Social Aspects of the Banana Industry.* New York, 1936.

11 KEPNER, C. D., and J. H. SOOTHILL. *The Banana Empire, A Case Study of Economic Imperialism.* New York, 1935.

12 LEWIS, Cleona. *America's Stake in International Investments.* Washington, D.C., 1938.

13 MUNRO, D. G. *The United States and the Caribbean Area.* Boston, 1934.

14 POWELL, F. W. *The Railroads of Mexico.* Boston, 1921.

15 REMER, C. F. *Foreign Investments in China.* New York, 1933.

16 RIPPY, J. F. *Latin America and the Industrial Age.* New York, 1944.

17 RIPPY, J. F. *The United States and Mexico.* New York, 1926.

18 SOUTHARD, F. A. *American Industry in Europe.* Boston and New York, 1931.

19 SPENCE, C. C. *British Investments and the American Mining Frontier.* Ithaca, N.Y., 1958.

20 SPENCE, C. C. "When the Pound Sterling Went West: British Investments and the American Mineral Frontier." *J Econ Hist*, XVI (1956), 482–492.

21 TURLINGTON, E. W. *Mexico and Her Foreign Creditors.* New York, 1930.

22 United States, Federal Trade Commission. *Report . . . on the Meat Packing Industry.* 6 vols. Pt. 1. Washington, D.C., 1919, pp. 160–199.

23 VEVIER, Charles. *The United States and China, 1906–1913.* New Brunswick, N.J., 1955.

V. Work, Wealth, and Welfare During the Fifty Years' War, 1914–1970

A. General Works

1 ALLEN, F. L. *The Big Change: America Transforms Itself, 1900–1950.* See 8.7.

2 ANDERSON, H. D. *Taxation, Recovery, and Defense.* Monograph 20, Temporary National Economic Committee (TNEC). Washington, D.C., 1940.

3 BALDWIN, W. L. *The Structure of the Defense Market.* Durham, N.C., 1967.

4 BELLUSH, Bernard. *Franklin D. Roosevelt as Governor of New York.* New York, 1955.

5 BIDDLE, F. B. *In Brief Authority.* Garden City, N.Y., 1962.

6 BLUM, J. M. *From the Morgenthau Diaries.* 3 vols. Boston, 1959–1967.

7 BOLTON, Roger E. *Defense Purchases and Regional Growth.* Washington, D.C., 1966.

8 BRAEMAN, J., R. H. BREMMER, and D. BRODY. *Change and Continuity in Twentieth-Century America: The 1920s.* Columbus, Ohio, 1968.†

9 FELS, Rendigs. "The U.S. Downturn of 1948." *Am Econ Rev,* LV (1965), 1059–1076.

10 FREIDEL, F. B. *Franklin D. Roosevelt.* 3 vols. Boston, 1952–1956.

11 FRIEDMAN, M., and A. J. SCHWARTZ. *The Great Contraction.* Princeton, 1965.†

12 GALBRAITH, J. K. *The Great Crash, 1929.* Boston, 1953.†

13 HARRIS, Seymour E. *Economics of the Kennedy Years, and a Look Ahead.* New York, 1964.

14 HODSON, H. V. *Slump and Recovery, 1929–1937. A Survey of World Economic Affairs.* London and New York, 1938.

15 HOOVER, Herbert. *American Individualism.* New York, 1923.

16 KARL, B. D. "Presidential Planning and Social Science Research: Mr. Hoover's Experts." *Pers Am Hist,* III (1969), 347–409.

17 KOHLMEIER, L. M., Jr. *The Regulators: Watchdog Agencies and the Public Interest.* New York, 1969.

1 KUZNETS, Simon. *Postwar Economic Growth, Four Lectures.* Cambridge, Mass., 1964.

2 LEUCHTENBERG, W. E. *Franklin D. Roosevelt and the New Deal, 1932–1940.* New York, 1963.†

3 LEUCHTENBERG, W. E. *The Perils of Prosperity, 1914–1932.* Chicago, 1958.†

4 MITCHELL, Broadus. *Depression Decade from New Era Through New Deal, 1929–1941.* New York, 1947.

5 MOLEY, Raymond. *After Seven Years.* New York and London, 1939.

6 MOLEY, Raymond. *The First New Deal.* New York, 1966.

7 NOSSITER, B. D. *The Mythmakers. An Essay on Power and Wealth.* Boston, 1964.†

8 PERKINS, Frances. *The Roosevelt I Knew.* New York, 1946.†

9 RICHBERG, Donald R. *My Hero: The Indiscreet Memoirs of an Eventful but Unheroic Life.* New York, 1954.

10 ROMASCO, A. U. *The Poverty of Abundance. Hoover, the Nation, the Depression.* New York, 1965.†

11 ROOSEVELT, F. D. *The Public Papers and Addresses of Franklin Delano Roosevelt.* Comp. by S. I. Rosenman. 13 vols. New York, 1938–1950.

12 SCHLESINGER, A. M., Jr. *The Age of Roosevelt.* 3 vols. Boston, 1957–1960.†

13 SMEAD, E. E. *Governmental Promotion and Regulation of Business.* New York, 1969.

14 SOULE, George. *Prosperity Decade; From War to Depression: 1917–1929.* New York, 1947.†

15 TINDALL, G. B. *The Emergence of the New South, 1913–1945.* Baton Rouge, 1967.

16 TOBIN, James. *National Economic Policy.* New Haven, Conn., 1966.

17 TUGWELL, R. G. *The Brain Trust.* New York, 1968.

18 TUGWELL, R. G. *The Democratic Roosevelt. A Biography of Franklin D. Roosevelt.* New York, 1957.†

19 United States, Committee on Recent Economic Changes of the President's Conference on Unemployment. *Recent Economic Changes in the United States.* 2 vols. New York, 1929.

20 United States, Federal Trade Commission. *Relative Efficiency of Large, Medium-Sized, and Small Business.* Monograph 13, Temporary National Economic Committee (TNEC). Washington, D.C., 1941.

21 VATTER, H. G. *The U.S. Economy in the 1950s.* New York, 1963.†

B. Manufacturing Technology

22 BARNOUW, Erik. *A History of Broadcasting in the United States.* 3 vols. New York, 1966–1970.

WORK, WEALTH, AND WELFARE, 1914–1970 **43**

1 BAUER, P. T. *The Rubber Industry. A Study in Competition and Monopoly.* Cambridge, Mass., 1948.

2 BIRR, K. A. "Science in American Industry." *Science and Society in the United States.* Ed. by D. D. Van Tassel and M. G. Hall.† See 20.2.

3 BRIGHT, A. A., Jr. *The Electric-Lamp Industry. Technological Change and Economic Development from 1800 to 1947.* New York, 1949.

4 BROEHL, W. G., Jr. *Precision Valley: The Machine Tool Companies of Springfield, Vermont.* Englewood Cliffs, N.J., 1959.

5 CLARK V. S. *History of Manufactures in the United States.* Vol. III. See 20.8.

6 DANHOF, C. H. *Government Contracting and Technological Change.* Washington, D.C., 1968.

7 FABRICANT, S. *The Output of Manufacturing Industries, 1899–1937.* See 20.13.

8 FUCHS, Victor R. "Some Implications of the Growing Importance of the Service Industries." National Bureau of Economic Research, *Forty-fifth Annual Report* (June, 1965), pp. 5–16.

9 GARVER, F. B., F. M. BODDY, and A. J. NIXON. *The Location of Manufactures in the United States, 1899–1929.* See 20.14.

10 GIBB, G. S. *The Saco-Lowell Shops: Textile Machinery Building in New England, 1813–1949.* See 20.15.

11 GIBB, G. S., and E. H. KNOWLTON. *History of Standard Oil Company (New Jersey). The Resurgent Years, 1911–1927.* New York, 1956, pp. 110–134, 320–569.

12 HAYNES. W. *American Chemical Industry.* 6 vols. New York, 1954.

13 KNOWLTON, E. H. *Pepperell's Progress: History of a Cotton Textile Company, 1844–1945.* See 21.1.

14 LINCOLN, S. B. *Lockwood Greene. The History of an Engineering Business, 1832–1958.* Brattleboro, Vt., 1960.

15 LORANT, J. H. "Technological Change in American Manufacturing During the 1920s." *J Econ Hist*, XXVII (1967), 243–246.

16 LORWIN, L. L., and J. M. BLAIR. *Technology in Our Economy.* Monograph 22, Temporary National Economic Committee (TNEC). Washington, D.C., 1941.

17 MAC LAURIN, W. R. *Invention and Innovation in the Radio Industry.* See 21.4.

18 MEAD, R. R. *An Analysis of the Decline of the Anthracite Industry Since 1921.* Philadelphia, 1935.

19 NAVIN, T. R. *The Whitin Machine Works Since 1831.* See 21.8.

20 NEVINS, Allan and F. E. HILL. *Ford.* 3 vols. New York, 1954–1963.

1 RAE, J. B. *American Automobile Manufacturers: The First Forty Years.* See 21.11.

2 RAE, J. B. *Climb to Greatness: The American Aircraft Industry, 1920–1960.* Cambridge, Mass., 1968.

3 ROSENBERG, N. "Technological Change in the Machine Tool Industry, 1840–1910." *J Econ Hist*, XXIII (1963), 414–446.

4 SCHMOOKIER, Jacob. "Technological Progress and the Modern American Corporation." *The Corporation in Modern Society.* Ed. by E. S. Mason. Cambridge, Mass., 1959.†

5 SIMONSON, G. R. "The Demand for Aircraft and the Aircraft Industry, 1907–1958." *J Econ Hist*, XX (1960), 361–382.

6 THOMPSON, G. V. "Intercompany Technical Standardization in the Early American Automobile Industry." *J Econ Hist*, XIV (1954), 1–20.

7 THORP, W. L. *The Integration of Industrial Operation.* See 21.17.

8 WAGONER, H. D. *The U.S. Machine Tool Industry from 1900 to 1950.* Cambridge, Mass., 1968.

C. The Organization of Business: Corporation and Consolidation

9 ADELMAN, M. A. "The Measurement of Industrial Concentration." *Rev Econ Stat*, XXXIII (1951), 269–296.

10 BERLE, A. A., Jr., and G. C. MEANS. *The Modern Corporation and Private Property.* New York, 1932.†

11 BERTRAND, D., W. D. EVANS, and E. L. BLANCHARD. *The Motion Picture Industry: A Pattern of Control.* Monograph 43, Temporary National Economic Committee (TNEC). Washington, D.C., 1941.

12 BURNS, A. R. *The Decline of Competition: A Study of the Evolution of American Industry.* New York, 1936.

13 CHANDLER, A. D. "The Beginnings of 'Big Business' in American History." *Bus Hist Rev*, XXXIII (1959), 1–31.

14 CHANDLER, A. D. *Strategy and Structure: Chapters in the History of the Industrial Enterprise.*† See 24.7.

15 COOK, R. C. *Control of the Petroleum Industry by Major Oil Companies.* Monograph 39, Temporary National Economic Committee (TNEC). Washington, D.C., 1941.

16 DANIELIAN, N. R. *A.T.&T. The Story of Industrial Conquest.* New York, 1939.

17 De CHAZEAU, M. G., and A. E. KAHN. *Integration and Competition in the Petroleum Industry.* New Haven, Conn., 1959.

18 EPSTEIN, E. M. *The Corporation in American Politics.* Englewood Cliffs, N.J., 1969.

19 FABRICANT, S. "Is Monopoly Increasing?" *J Econ Hist*, XIII (1953), 89–94.

1 FISHER, B. R., and S. B. WITHEY. *Big Business as the People See It. A Study of a Socio-Economic Institution.* Ann Arbor, Mich., 1951.

2 GALAMBOS, Louis. *Competition & Cooperation; The Emergence of a National Trade Association.* Baltimore, 1966.

3 GIBB, G. S., and E. H. KNOWLTON. *History of Standard Oil Company (New Jersey). The Resurgent Years. 1918–1927.* See 43.11.

4 HOFFMAN, A. C. *Large-Scale Organization in the Food Industries.* Monograph 35, Temporary National Economic Committee (TNEC). Washington, D.C., 1940.

5 HOUGHTON, H. F. "The Progress of Concentration in Industry. The Growth of Big Business." *Am Econ Rev, Papers and Proceedings,* XXXVIII (1948), 72–120.

6 KIRKENDALL, R. S. "A. A. Berle, Jr., Student of the Corporation, 1917–1932." *Bus Hist Rev,* XXXV (1961), 43–58.

7 MASON, E. S. *Economic Concentration and the Monopoly Problem.* Cambridge, Mass., 1957.

8 MASON, E. S., ed. *The Corporation in Modern Society.* Cambridge, Mass., 1960.†

9 MASSELL, M. S. *Competition and Monopoly.* Washington, D.C., 1962.

10 MITCHELL, S. A. *S. Z. Mitchell and the Electrical Industry.* New York 1960.

11 NELSON, R. L. *Merger Movements in American Industry, 1895–1956.* Princeton, 1959.

12 NUTTER, G. W., and H. A. EINHORN. *Enterprise Monopoly in the United States, 1899–1958.* New York, 1969.

13 PECK, Merton J. *Competition in the Aluminum Industry, 1945–1958.* Cambridge, Mass., 1961.

14 STIGLER, G. J. "Monopoly and Oligopoly by Merger." *Am Econ Rev, Papers and Proceedings,* XL (1950), 23–34.

15 THORP, W. L., W. E. CROWDER, and associates. *The Structure of Industry.* Monograph 27, Temporary National Economic Committee (TNEC). Washington, D.C., 1941.

16 WILCOX, C. *Competition and Monopoly in American Industry.* Monograph 21, Temporary National Economic Committee (TNEC). Washington, D.C., 1940.

17 WILCOX, C. "On the Alleged Ubiquity of Oligopoly." *Am Econ Rev, Papers and Proceedings,* XL (1950), 67–73.

D. New Phases of Antitrust

18 American Bar Association, Section on Antitrust Law. *Antitrust Developments, 1955–1968.* n.p., 1968.

19 ARNOLD, T. W. *The Bottlenecks of Business.* New York, 1940.

1 BAIN, J. S. *Barriers to New Competition*. Cambridge, Mass., 1956.

2 BURNS, J. W. *A Study of the Antitrust Laws*. New York, 1958.

3 CARROTT, M. B. "The Supreme Court and American Trade Associations, 1921–1925." *Bus Hist Rev*, XLIV (1970), 320–338.

4 CONANT, M. *Antitrust in the Motion Picture Industry*. Berkeley, 1960.

5 DAVIS, G. C. "The Transformation of the Federal Trade Commission, 1914–1929." *Miss Val Hist Rev*, XLIX (1962), 437–445.

6 EDWARDS, C. D. *Maintaining Competition; Requisites of a Governmental Policy*. New York, 1949.

7 GRESSLEY, G. M. "Thurman Arnold, Antitrust and the New Deal." *Bus Hist Rev*, XXXVIII (1964), 214–231.

8 HAMILTON, W., and Irene TILL. *Antitrust in Action*. Monograph 16, Temporary National Economic Committee (TNEC). Washington, 1940.

9 HANDLER, M. *A Study of the Construction and Enforcement of the Federal Antitrust Laws*. See 27.6.

10 HAWLEY, E. W. *The New Deal and the Problem of Monopoly: A Study in Economic Ambivalence*. Princeton, 1966.†

11 KAYSEN, C., and D. F. TURNER. *Antitrust Policy*. Cambridge, Mass., 1959.

12 KEEZER, D. M., ed. "The Effectiveness of the Federal Antitrust Laws: A Symposium." *Am Econ Rev*, XXXIX (1949), 689–724.

13 KLEBANER, B. J. "Potential Competition and the American Antitrust Legislation of 1914." *Bus Hist Rev*, XXXVIII (1964), 163–185.

14 MARTIN, D. D. "The Brown Shoe Case and the New Antimerger Policy." *Am Econ Rev*, LIII (June 1963), 340–358.

15 MARTIN, D. D. *Mergers and the Clayton Act*. Berkeley and Los Angeles, 1959.

16 NEALE, A. D. *The Antitrust Laws of the United States of America. A Study of Competition Enforced by Law*. See 27.10.

17 NELSON, S., W. G. KEIM, and E. S. MASON. *Price Behavior and Business Policy*. Monograph 1, Temporary National Economic Committee (TNEC). Washington, D.C., 1940.

18 PHILLIPS, Almarin, ed. *Perspectives on Antitrust Policy*. Princeton, 1965.

19 PURDY, H. L., M. L. LINDAHL, and W. A. CARTER. *Corporate Concentration and Public Policy*. 2d ed. Englewood Cliffs, N.J., 1950.

1 ROSTOW, E. V. *Planning for Freedom—the Public Law of American Capitalism.* New Haven, Conn., 1959.†

2 STOCKING, G. W., and M. W. WATKINS. *Monopoly and Free Enterprise.* New York, 1951.

3 United States, Federal Trade Commission. *The Basing Point Problem.* Monograph 42, Temporary National Economic Committee (TNEC). Washington, D.C., 1941.

4 UROFSKY, M. I. *Big Steel and the Wilson Administration: A Study in Business-Government Relations.* Columbus, Ohio, 1969.

E. Government Planning, Control, and Ownership

5 BAILEY, S. K. *Congress Makes a Law. The Story Behind the Employment Act of 1946.* New York, 1950.

6 BAKER, R. H. *The National Bituminous Coal Commission. Administration of the Bituminous Coal Act, 1937–1941.* Baltimore, 1941.

7 BARTLEY, E. R. *The Tidelands Oil Controversy. A Legal and Historical Analysis.* Austin, 1953.

8 BERNSTEIN, M. H. *Regulating Business by Independent Commission.* Princeton, 1955.

9 CANTERBURY, E. R. *The President's Council of Economic Advisers: A Study of Its Functions and Its Influence on the Chief Executive's Decisions.* New York, 1961.

10 CANTERBURY, Ray. *Economics on a New Frontier.* Belmont, Calif., 1969.

11 CAVES, R. E. *Air Transport and Its Regulators.* Cambridge, Mass., 1962.

12 Chamber of Commerce, United States. *Government Competition, Problem and Perspective.* Washington, D.C., 1954.

13 CLAPP, G. B. *The TVA: An Approach to the Development of a Region.* Chicago, 1955.

14 COOPER, Henry S. F. *Apollo on the Moon.* New York, 1969.

15 DE BEDTS, Ralph F. *The New Deal, SEC: The Formative Years.* New York, 1964.

16 EMERY, W. B. *Broadcasting and Government.* East Lansing, Mich., 1961.

17 FINE, Sidney. *The Automobile Under the Blue Eagle; Labor, Management and the Automobile Manufacturing Code.* Ann Arbor, Mich., 1963.

18 FISHER, R. M. *Twenty Years of Public Housing: Economic Aspects of the Federal Program.* New York, 1959.

19 FLASH, E. S., Jr. *Economic Advice and Presidential Leadership. The Council of Economic Advisors.* New York, 1965.

20 GLAESER, M. G. *Public Utilities in American Capitalism.* New York, 1957.

1 HELLER, Walter W. *New Dimensions of Political Economy.* Cambridge, Mass., 1966.†

2 HERRING, J. M., and G. C. GROSS. *Telecommunications, Economics and Regulation.* New York, 1936.

3 HODGETTS, J. E. *Administering the Atom for Peace.* New York, 1964.

4 HUBBARD, P. J. *Origins of the T.V.A. The Muscle Shoals Controversy, 1920–1932.* Nashville, 1968.†

5 JOHNSON, A. M. *Petroleum Pipelines and Public Policy, 1906–1959.* Cambridge, Mass., 1967.

6 JOHNSON, J. P. "Drafting the NRA Code of Fair Competition for the Bituminous Coal Industry." *Miss Val Hist Rev,* LIII (1966), 521–541.

7 KING, J. *The Conservation Fight.* Washington, D.C., 1959.

8 KLEINSORGE, P. L. *The Boulder Canyon Project.* Stanford, 1941.

9 KOHLMEIER, L. M. *The Regulators. Watchdog Agencies and the Public Interest.* See 41.18.

10 LEVIN, H. J. *Broadcast Regulation and Joint Ownership of Media.* New York, 1960.

11 LILLIENTHAL, D. E. *TVA: Democracy on the March.* New York, 1944.

12 LYON, L. S., et al. *The National Recovery Administration. An Analysis and Appraisal.* Washington, D.C., 1935.

13 Mc KINLEY, C. *Uncle Sam in the Pacific Northwest.* Berkeley, 1952.

14 MULLER, F. W. *Public Rural Electrification.* Washington, D.C., 1944.

15 NASH, G. D. *United States Oil Policy, 1890–1964: Business and Government in Twentieth Century America.* Pittsburgh, 1968.

16 NELSON, J. C., E. W. WILLIAMS, Jr., and S. BERGE. "Changes in National Transportation Policy." *Am Econ Rev, Papers and Proceedings,* XLI (1950), 495–537.

17 NEVINS, Allan, and F. E. HILL. *Ford: Decline and Rebirth, 1933–1962.* New York, 1963.

18 NOURSE, E. G. *Economics in the Public Service. Administrative Aspects of the Employment Act.* Washington, D.C., 1953.

19 PETERSON, W. H. *The Question of Governmental Oil Import Restrictions.* Washington, D.C., 1959.

20 PRITCHETT, C. H. *The Tennessee Valley Authority.* Chapel Hill, N.C., 1943.

21 RATCHFORD, B. U. "Government Action or Private Enterprise in River Valley Development: An Economist's View." *Am Econ Rev, Papers and Proceedings,* XLI (1951), 299–306.

22 RAVER, P. J. "Government Action and Private Enterprise in River Valley Development. A Public Administrator's View." *Am Econ Rev, Papers and Proceedings,* XLI (1951), 289–298.

1   RIDGEWAY, M. E. *The Missouri Basin's Pick-Sloan Plan*. Urbana, Ill., 1955.

2   RITCHIE, R. F. *Integration of Public Utility Holding Companies*. Ann Arbor, Mich., 1955.

3   ROOS, C. F. *NRA Economic Planning*. Bloomington, Ind., 1937.

4   ROSTOW, E. V. *Planning for Freedom—The Public Law of American Capitalism*. New Haven, Conn., 1939.

5   SCHULTZ, G. P., and R. Z. ALIBER, eds. *Guidelines, Informal Controls, and the Market Place: Policy Choices in a Full Employment Economy*. Chicago, 1966.

6   SLESINGER, R. E., ed. *National Economic Policy; The Presidential Reports*. Princeton, 1968.†

7   STRAUSS, Lewis L. *Men and Decisions*. Garden City, N.Y., 1962.

8   THAYER, F. C., Jr. *Air Transport Policy and National Security*. Chapel Hill, N.C., 1965.

9   THOMAS, Morgan. *Atomic Energy and Congress*. Ann Arbor, Mich., 1956.

10 WATKINS, M. W. *Oil: Stabilization or Conservation*. New York, 1937.

11 WHITNAH, D. R. *Safer Skyways: Federal Control of Aviation, 1926–1966*. Ames, Iowa, 1966.

12 WILDAVSKY, A. *Dixon Yates: A Study in Power Politics*. New Haven, Conn., 1962.

13 WILEY, H. W. *An Autobiography*. Indianapolis, 1930.

14 WILLIAMSON, H. F., et al. *The American Petroleum Industry*. 2 vols. Evanston, Ill., 1959–1963. Vol. II, pp. 535–566.

15 WILSON, S. *Food and Drug Regulation*. Washington, D.C., 1942.

F.   Mobilization for World War I

16 BEAVER, D. R. *Newton D. Baker and the American War Effort, 1917–1918*. Lincoln, Neb., 1966.

17 CLARK, J. M. *The Costs of the World War to the American People*. New Haven, Conn., and London, 1931.

18 CLARKSON, G. B. *Industrial America in the World War: The Strategy Behind the Line, 1917–1918*. Boston and New York, 1923.

19 CUFF, R. D. "Bernard Baruch: Symbol and Myth in Industrial Mobilization." *Bus Hist Rev*, XLIII (1969), 115–133.

20 FULLER, J. V. "Genesis of the Munitions Traffic." *J Mod Hist*, VI (1934), 280–293.

21 HINES, W. D. *War History of American Railroads*. New Haven, Conn., and London, 1928.

1 HURLEY, E. N. *The Bridge to France*. Philadelphia and London, 1927.

2 KERR, K. A. "Decision for Federal Control: Wilson, McAdoo, and the Railroads, 1917." *J Am Hist*, LIV (1967), 550–560.

3 KOISTINEN, P. A. C. "The 'Industrial Military Complex' in Historical Perspective: World War I." *Bus Hist Rev*, XLI (1967), 378–403.

4 Mc ADOO, W. G. *Crowded Years: The Reminiscences of William G. McAdoo*. Boston and New York, 1931.

5 MULLENDORE, W. C. *History of the United States Food Administration, 1917–1919*. Stanford, 1941.

6 NOYES, A. D. *The War Period of American Finance*. New York, 1926.

7 PHILLIPS, E. C. "American Participation in Belligerent Commercial Controls 1914–1917." *Am J Int Law*, XXVII (1933), 675–693.

8 ROSE, J. R. *American Wartime Transportation*. New York, 1953.

9 SURFACE, F. M., and R. L. BLAND. *American Food in the World War and Reconstruction Period: Operations of the Organizations Under the Direction of Herbert Hoover, 1914 to 1924*. Stanford, 1931.

10 TANSILL, C. C. *America Goes to War*. Boston, 1938, pp. 32–133, 188–224, 660–663.

11 VAN ALSTYNE, R. W. "Private American Loans to the Allies 1914–1916." *Pac Hist Rev*, II (1933), 180–193.

12 WATKINS, G. S. *Labor Problems and Labor Administration in the United States During the World War*. 2 vols. University of Illinois Studies in the Social Sciences, VIII, nos. 3–4. Urbana, Ill., 1920.

13 WOLFE, A. B., and Helen OLSON. "War-Time Industrial Employment of Women in the United States." *J Pol Econ*, XXVII (1919), 639–669.

G.   Mobilization for World War II

14 BAXTER, J. P., III. *Scientists Against Time*. Boston, 1946.†

15 BERNSTEIN, B. J. "The Removal of War Production Board Controls on Business, 1944–1946." *Bus Hist Rev*, XXIX (1965), 243–260.

16 BUSH, Vannever. *Science: The Endless Frontier. A Report to the President*. Washington, D.C., 1945.

17 GROVES, Leslie R. *Now It Can Be Told. The Story of Manhattan Project*. New York, 1962.

18 HEWLETT, R. G., and Oscar H. ANDERSON, Jr. *The New World, 1939–1946*. University Park, Pa., 1962.

19 JANEWAY, Eliot. *The Struggle for Survival: A Chronicle of Economic Mobilization in World War II*. New Haven, Conn., 1951.

1   KAPLAN, A. D. H. *The Liquidation of War Production.* New York, 1944.

2   KOISTINEN, P. A. C. "The 'Industrial-Military Complex' in Historical Perspective: The InterWar Years." *J Am Hist*, LVI (1970), 819–839.

3   LANE, F. C. *Ships for Victory: A History of Shipbuilidng Under the U.S. Maritime Commission in World War II.* Baltimore, 1951.

4   MANSFIELD, H. C., and associates. *A Short History of OPA.* Washington, D.C., 1947.

5   MILLER, J. P. "Military Procurement Policies: World War II and Today." *Am Econ Rev, Papers and Proceedings*, XLII (1952), 451–475.

6   NELSON, Donald M. *Arsenal of Democracy. The Story of American War Production.* New York, 1946.

7   NOVICK, D., M. ANSHEN, and W. C. TRUPPNER. *Wartime Production Controls.* New York, 1949.

8   SOMERS, H. M. *Presidential Agency: OWMR. The Office of War Mobilization and Reconversion.* Cambridge, Mass., 1950.

9   STEIN, Bruno. "Labor's Role in Government Agencies During World War II." *J Econ Hist*, XVII (1957), 389–408.

10   STROMBERG, R. N. "American Business and the Approach of War, 1935–1941." *J Econ Hist*, XIII (1953), 58–78.

11   United States, Bureau of Demobilization, Civilian Production Administration. *Industrial Mobilization for War. History of the War Production Board and Predecessor Agencies, 1940–1945.* Washington, D.C., 1947.

12   United States, Department of Interior. *History of the Petroleum Administration for War.* Washington, D.C., 1946.

13   United States, National War Labor Board. *The Termination Report.* Vol. I. Washington, D.C., 1949.

14   WHITE, G. T. "Financing Industrial Expansion for War: The Origin of the Defense Plant Corporation Leases." *J Econ Hist*, XIX (1959), 156–183.

H.   *Agriculture Since 1914*

15   BAKER, Gladys L. *The County Agent.* Chicago, 1939.

16   BENSON, Ezra T. *Cross Fire: Eight Years with Eisenhower.* Garden City, N.Y., 1963.

17   BLACK, John D. *The Dairy Industry and the AAA.* Washington, D.C., 1935.

1 CAMPBELL, C. M. *The Farm Bureau and the New Deal: A Study of Making of National Farm Policy, 1933–1940.* Urbana, Ill., 1962.

2 CASE, H. C. M. "Farm Debt Adjustment During the Early 1930s." *Ag Hist*, XXXIV (1960), 173–181.

3 CONNOR, J. R. "National Farm Organizations and United States Tariff Policy in the 1920s." *Ag Hist*, XXXII (1958), 32–43.

4 CONRAD, David E. *The Forgotten Farmers: The Story of Sharecroppers in the New Deal.* Urbana, Ill., 1965.

5 DAVIS, C. C. "The Development of Agricultural Policy Since the End of the World War." *Farmers in a Changing World: The Yearbook of Agriculture, 1940*, U.S. Department of Agriculture. Washington, D.C., 1940, pp. 297–326.

6 FITE, G. C. "Farmer Opinion and the Agricultural Adjustment Act, 1933." *Miss Val Hist Rev*, LXVIII (1962), 656–673.

7 FITE, G. C. *George N. Peek and the Fight for Farm Parity.* Norman, Okla., 1954.

8 FITE, G. C. "John A. Simpson: The Southwest's Militant Farm Leader." *Miss Val Hist Rev*, XXXV (1949), 563–584.

9 GALBRAITH, J. K. "Economic Preconceptions and the Farm Policy." *Am Econ Rev*, XLIV (1954), 40–52.

10 GENUNG, A. B. "Agriculture in the World War [I] Period." *Farmers in a Changing World: The Yearbook of Agriculture, 1940*, U.S. Department of Agriculture. Washington, D.C., 1940, pp. 277–295.

11 GLEASON, J. P. "The Attitude of the Business Community Toward Agriculture During the McNary-Haugen Period." *Ag Hist*, XXXII (1958), 127–138.

12 HATHAWAY, Dale E. *Government and Agriculture. Public Policy in a Democratic Society.* New York, 1963.

13 HICKS, J. D., and T. SALOUTOS. *Agricultural Discontent in the Middle West, 1900–1939.* Madison, Wis., 1951.

14 HOOVER, H. C. *The Memoirs of Herbert Hoover. Years of Adventure, 1874–1920.* New York, 1951–1953.

15 JENNY, Hans. *E. W. Hilgard and the Birth of Modern Soil Science.* Pisa, Italy, 1961.

16 JOHNSON, D. G. "Competition in Agriculture: Fact or Fiction." *Am Econ Rev, Papers and Proceedings*, XLIV (1954), 107–115.

17 JOHNSON, W. R. "National Farm Organizations and the Reshaping of Agricultural Policy in 1932." *Ag Hist*, XXXVII (1963), 35–42.

18 JONES, C. C. "The Burlington Railroad and Agricultural Policy in the 1920s." *Ag Hist*, XXXI (October, 1957), 67–74.

19 KILE, O. M. *The Farm Bureau Through Three Decades.* Baltimore, 1948.

20 KIRKENDALL, R. S. "Howard Tolley and Agricultural Planning in the 1930s." *Ag Hist*, XXXIX (1965), 25–33.

1 KIRKENDALL, R. S. "L. C. Gray and the Supply of Agricultural Land." (Comments by Paul Gates) *Ag Hist*, XXXVII (1963), 206–216.

2 KIRKENDALL, R. S. *Social Scientists and Farm Politics in the Age of Roosevelt*. Columbia, Mo., 1966.

3 KNAPP, J. G. *The Hard Winter Wheat Pools: An Experiment in Agricultural Marketing Integration*. Chicago, 1933.

4 LAMER, Mirko. *The World Fertilizer Economy*. Stanford, 1957.

5 Mc GOVERN, George S. *War Against Want: America's Food For Peace Program*. New York, 1964.

6 MARTIN, R. E. "The Referendum Process in the Agricultural Adjustment Programs of the United States." *Ag Hist*, XXV (1951), 34–47.

7 MATUSOW, A. J. *Farm Policies and Politics in the Truman Years* Cambridge, Mass., 1967.

8 MORLAN, R. L. *Political Prairie Fire: The Nonpartisan League, 1915–1922*. Minneapolis, 1955.

9 PEARSON, F. A., W. I. MYERS, and A. R. GANS. "Warren as Presidential Advisor." *Farm Economics*, CCXI (December, 1957), 5597–5676.

10 PERKINS, V. L. *Crisis in Agriculture: The Agricultural Adjustment Administration and the New Deal, 1933*. Berkeley and Los Angeles, 1969.

11 PETERSON, W. H. *The Great Farm Problem*. Chicago, 1959.

12 ROWLEY, W. D. *M. L. Wilson and the Campaign for the Domestic Allotment*. Lincoln, Neb., 1970.

13 SCHAPSMEIER, E. L. and F. H. *Henry A. Wallace of Iowa. The Agrarian Years, 1910–1940*. Ames, Iowa, 1968.

14 SCHLEBECKER, John T. *Cattle Raising on the Plains, 1900–1961*. Lincoln, Neb., 1963.

15 SHIDELER, J. H. "The Development of the Parity Price Formula for Agriculture, 1919–1923." *Ag Hist*, XXVII (1953), 77–84.

16 SHIDELER, J. H. *Farm Crisis, 1919–1923*. Berkeley and Los Angeles, 1957.

17 SHOVER, J. L. *Cornbelt Rebellion: The Farmers' Holiday Association*. Urbana, Ill., 1965.

18 SHOVER, J. L. "Populism in the Nineteen-Thirties; The Battle for the AAA." *Ag Hist*, XXXIX (1965), 17–24.

19 SLICHTER, G. A. "Franklin D. Roosevelt's Farm Policy as Governor of New York State, 1928–1932." *Ag Hist*, XXXIII (1959), 167–176.

20 SOTH, Lauren. *Farm Trouble*. Princeton, 1961.

21 TONTZ, R. L. "Origin of the Base Period Concept of Parity—A Significant Value Judgment in Agricultural Policy." *Ag Hist*, XXXII (1958), 3–13.

1 TUCKER, W. P. "Populism Up-to-Date: The Story of the Farmers' Union." *Ag Hist*, XXI (1947), 198–208.

2 TUGWELL, R. G. "The Resettlement Idea." *Ag Hist*, XXXIII (1959), 159–164.

3 United States, Department of Agriculture. *Farmer's World: The Yearbook of Agriculture, 1964.* Washington, D.C., 1964.

4 VANCE, R. B. *Human Geography of the South.* Chapel Hill, N.C., 1932.

5 VANCE, R. B., and C. S. JOHNSON. *The Collapse of Cotton Tenancy.* Chapel Hill, N.C., 1935.

I. Labor Since 1914

1. GENERAL WORKS

6 BERNSTEIN, Irving. *The Lean Years—A History of the American Worker, 1920–1933.* Boston, 1960.

7 BERNSTEIN, Irving. *Turbulent Years: A History of the American Worker, 1933–1941.* Boston, 1969.

8 DERBER, Milton, and Edwin YOUNG, eds. *Labor and the New Deal.* Madison, Wis., 1957.

9 EILBERT, Henry. "The Development of Personnel Management in the United States." *Bus Hist Rev*, XXXIII (1959), 345–364.

10 LEBERGOTT, Stanley. *Manpower in Economic Growth. The American Record Since 1800.* See 3.10.

11 SEIDMAN, J. *American Labor from Defense to Reconversion.* Chicago, 1953.

2. CONSTITUENTS OF THE LABOR FORCE

12 BANCROFT, Gertrude. *The American Labor Force.* See 28.2.

13 BERTHOFF, R. T. *British Immigrants in Industrial America, 1790–1950.* See 28.3.

14 COLE, D. B. *Immigrant City: Lawrence, Massachusetts, 1845–1921.* Chapel Hill, N.C., 1963.

15 DURAND, J. D. *The Labor Force in the United States, 1890–1960.* See 28.5.

16 FOERSTER, R. F. *The Italian Emigration of Our Times.* See 28.7.

17 HEALD, M. "Business Attitudes Toward European Immigration." See 28.11.

18 HILL, J. A. *Women in Gainful Occupations, 1870–1920.* See 28.12.

1 JEROME, Harry. *Migrations and Business Cycles.* See 28.13.

2 KENNEDY, L. V. *The Negro Peasant Turns Cityward.* See 28.15.

3 KUZNETS, Simon, and D. S. THOMAS. *Population Redistribution and Economic Growth in the United States, 1870–1950.* See 28.16.

4 MILLER, A. R. "Components of Labor Force Growth." See 28.18.

5 SPERO, S. D., and A. L. HARRIS. *The Black Worker. The Negro and the Labor Movement.* New York, 1931.†

6 United States, Congress, Senate. *Report on Condition of Women and Child Wage-earners . . .* 61st Cong., 2nd Sess. Senate Doc. No. 645. See 29.2.

7 United States, Immigration Commission. *Reports.* See 29.1.

8 WOODSON, C. G. *A Century of Negro Migration.* See 29.3.

3. LABOR ORGANIZATION

9 BERNSTEIN, Irving. "The Growth of American Unions." *Am Econ Rev,* XLIV (1954), 301–318.

10 BRODY, David. *Labor in Crisis: The Steel Strike of 1919.* Philadelphia, 1965.

11 FONER, P. S. *History of the Labor Movement in the United States.* 4 vols. New York, 1947–1965.

12 FRIEDHEIM, R. L. *The Seattle General Strike.* Seattle, 1964.

13 GOLDBERG, A. J. *AFL-CIO: Labor United.* New York, 1956.

14 JAMES, Ralph, and Estelle JAMES. *Hoffa and the Teamsters—A Study of Union Power.* Princeton, 1965.

15 MORRIS, James O. *Conflict Within the AFL: A Study of Craft Versus Industrial Unionism, 1901–1938.* Ithaca, N.Y., 1958.

16 PERLMAN, Selig. "Upheaval and Reorganization (Since 1876)." Vol. II of *History of Labour in the United States,* by J. R. Commons et al. New York, 1918.

17 PERLMAN, Selig, and Philip TAFT. "Labor Movements." Vol. IV of *History of Labor in the United States,* by J. R. Commons et al. New York, 1935.

18 SHANNON, D. A. *The Decline of American Communism: A History of the Communist Party of the United States Since 1945.* New York, 1959.

19 STALEY, E. *History of the Illinois State Federation of Labor.* See 31.20.

20 TAFT, Philip. *The A.F. of L. in the Time of Gompers.* See 32.2.

1 TAFT, Philip. *The A.F. of L. from the Death of Gompers to the Merger.* See 32.1.

2 WOLMAN, Leo. *The Growth of American Trade Unions.* See 32.4.

4. THE RIGHT TO RECOGNITION

3 AUERBACH, J. S. *Labor and Liberty: The La Follette Committee and the New Deal.* Indianapolis, 1966.

4 BERNSTEIN, Irving. *The New Deal Collective Bargaining Policy.* Berkeley, 1950.

5 BRODY, D. "The Rise and Decline of Welfare Capitalism." *Change and Continuity in Tewntieth-Century America. The 1920s.* Ed. by J. Braeman. Columbus, Ohio, 1968.†

6 DERBER, M., and E. YOUNG, eds. *Labor and the New Deal.* See 54.8.

7 FINE, Sidney. *The Automobile Under the Blue Eagle. Labor, Management and the Automobile Manufacturing Code.* Ann Arbor, Mich., 1963.

8 FINE, Sidney. *Sit-Down: The General Motors Strike of 1936–1937.* Ann Arbor, Mich., 1969.

9 HOFFMAN, C. E. *Sit-Down in Anderson: U.A.W., Local 663, Anderson, Indiana.* Detroit, 1968.

10 LEE, R. A. *Truman and Taft-Hartley: A Question of Mandate.* Lexington, Ky., 1966.

11 MILLIS, H. A., and E. C. BROWN. *From the Wagner Act to Taft-Hartley. A Study of National Labor Policy and Labor Relations.* Chicago, 1950.

12 NEVINS, Allan, and F. E. HILL. *Ford: Decline and Rebirth.* See 39.10.

13 POMPER, Gerald. "Labor and Congress: The Repeal of Taft-Hartley." *Labor History,* II (1961), 323–343.

14 WAKSTEIN, A. M. "The Origins of the Open-Shop Movement, 1919–1920." *Miss Val Hist Rev,* LI (1964), 460–475.

5. LABOR CONDITIONS

15 KUCZYNSKI, Jürgen. *A Short History of Labour Conditions Under Industrial Capitalism.* See 29.12.

16 LESCOHIER, D. D. "Working Conditions." Vol. III of *History of Labor in the United States,* by J. R. Commons et al. See 29.13.

6. LABOR AND THE GOVERNMENT

17 BERMAN, E. *Labor and the Sherman Act.* New York and London, 1930.

1 BLACKMAN, J. L., Jr. *Presidential Seizure in Labor Disputes.* Cambridge, Mass., 1967.

2 BRANDEIS, E. "Labor Legislation." Vol. III of *History of Labor in the United States*, by J. R. Commons et al. See 34.1.

3 Mc CLURE, A. F. *The Truman Administration and the Problems of Post-War Labor, 1945–1948.* Cranbury, N.J., 1969.

4 MORTON, Herbert C. *Public Contracts and Private Wages: Experience Under the Walsh-Healey Act.* Washington, D.C., 1965.†

5 NASH, G. D. "Franklin D. Roosevelt and Labor: The World War I Origins of Early New Deal Policy." *Labor History*, I (1960), 39–52.

6 TAYLOR, A. G. *Labor and the Supreme Court.* Ann Arbor, Mich., 1958.

7 ZIEGER, R. H. "From Hostility to Moderation: Railroad Labor Policy in the 1920s." *Labor History*, IX (1968), 23–38.

8 ZIEGER, R. H. *Republicans and Labor, 1919–1929.* Lexington, Ky., 1969.

7. SOCIAL SECURITY

9 HABER, William, and Merrill G. MURRAY. *Unemployment Insurance in the American Economy.* Homewood, Ill., 1966.

10 LUBOVE, Roy. *The Struggle for Social Security, 1900–1935.* Cambridge, Mass., 1968.

11 NELSON, Daniel. *Unemployment Insurance: The American Experience, 1915–1935.* Madison, Wis., 1969.

12 ROBINOW, I. M. *The Quest for Security.* New York, 1934.

13 WITTE, E. E. *The Development of the Social Security Act.* Madison, Wis., 1962.†

14 WITTE, E. E. *Social Security Perspectives. Essays.* Ed. by R. J. Lampman. Madison, Wis., 1962.

J. Methods and Means of Fiscal-Monetary Direction

15 BLAKEY, R. G. and G. C. "The Revenue Act of 1935." *Am Econ Rev*, XXV (1935), 673–690.

16 BLAKEY, R. G. and G. C. "The Two Federal Revenue Acts of 1940." *Am Econ Rev*, XXX (1940), 724–735.

17 BUTTERS, J. K. "Taxation, Incentives, and Financial Capacity." *Am Econ Rev, Papers and Proceedings*, XLIV (1954), 504–519.

18 CHANDLER, L. V. *Benjamin Strong, Central Banker.* Washington, D.C., 1958.

1 CLIFFORD, A. J. *The Independence of the Federal Reserve System.* Philadelphia, 1965.

2 COWING, C. B. *Populists, Plungers, and Progressives. A Social History of Stock and Commodity Speculation, 1890–1936.* Princeton, 1968.†

3 ECCLES, Marriner S. *Beckoning Frontiers. Public and Personal Recollections.* Ed. by S. Hyman. New York, 1951.

4 FRIEDMAN, M., and A. J. SCHWARTZ. *A Monetary History of the United States.* See 41.12.

5 GOLDENWEISER, E. A. *American Monetary Policy.* New York, 1951.

6 HOLMANS, A. E. *United States Fiscal Policy 1945–1959. Its Contribution to Economic Stability.* London, 1961.

7 PARIS, J. D. *Monetary Policies of the United States, 1932–1938.* New York, 1938.

8 STEIN, Herbert. *The Fiscal Revolution in America.* Chicago, 1969.

9 WICKER, E. R. *Federal Reserve Monetary Policy, 1917–1933.* New York, 1966.

10 WOLF, H. A. *Monetary and Fiscal Policy.* Columbus, Ohio, 1966.

K. Transportation

11 ARTH, M. P. "Federal Transport Regulatory Policy." *Am Econ Rev, Papers and Proceedings*, LII (1962), 416–435.

12 CAVES, R. E. *Air Transport and Its Regulators. An Industry Study.* Cambridge, Mass., 1962.

13 DAVIES, R. E. *The World's Airlines.* New York, 1964.

14 DEARING, C. L. *American Highway Policy.* Washington, D.C., 1941.

15 DEARING, C. L., and Wilfred OWEN. *National Transportation Policy.* Washington, D.C., 1949.

16 DIMOCK, M. E. *Developing America's Waterways.* Chicago, 1935.

17 FULDA, C. H. *Competition in the Regulated Industries. Transportation.* Boston, 1961.

18 FULLER, W. E. "Good Roads and Rural Free Delivery of Mail." *Miss Val Hist Rev*, XLII (1955), 67–83.

19 HILTON, G. W. *The Transportation Act of 1958: A Decade of Experience.* Bloomington, Ind., 1969.

20 HILTON, G. W., and J. F. DEW. *The Electric Interurban Railways in America.* Stanford, 1960.

21 HUTCHINS, J. G. B. "The Effect of the Civil War and the Two World Wars on American Transportation." *Am Econ Rev, Papers and Proceedings*, XLII (1952), 626–638.

1 JOHNSON, A. M. *The Development of American Petroleum Pipelines.* Ithaca, N.Y., 1956.

2 JOSEPHSON, M. *Empire of the Air: Juan Trippe and the Struggle for World Airways.* New York, 1943–1944.

3 KERR, K. A. *American Railroad Politics, 1914–1920: Rates, Wages, and Efficiency.* Pittsburgh, 1968.

4 MASON, E. S. *The Street Railway in Massachusetts; The Rise and Decline of an Industry.* Cambridge, Mass., 1932.

5 MEYER, J. R., J. F. KAIN, and M. WOHL. *The Urban Transportation Problem.* Cambridge, Mass., 1965.

6 NORTON, Hugh S. *National Transportation Policy: Formation and Implementation.* Berkeley, 1967.

7 RAE, J. B. "Financial Problems of the American Aircraft Industry. 1906–1940." *Bus Hist Rev*, XXXIX (1965), 99–114.

8 RICHMOND, S. B. *Regulation and Competition in Air Transportation.* New York, 1961.

9 ROBERTS, M. J. "The Motor Transportation Revolution." *Bus Hist Rev*, XXX (1956), 57–95.

10 SMITH, H. L. *Airways, The History of Commercial Aviation in the United States.* New York, 1942.

11 United States, Presidential Advisory Committee on Transport Policy and Organization. *Revision of Federal Transportation Policy. A Report to the President.* Washington, D.C., 1955.

12 WILCOX, D. F. *Analysis of the Electric Railway Problem; Report to the Federal Electric Railways Commission.* New York, 1921.

13 WILLOUGHBY, W. R. *The St. Lawrence Waterway.* Madison, Wis., 1961.

14 WILSON, E. E. *Kitty Hawk to Sputnik to Polaris.* Barre, Mass., 1960.

L. International Trade, Investment, and Aid

15 ACHESON, Dean. *Present at the Creation.* New York, 1969.

16 BALDWIN, David A. *Economic Development and American Foreign Policy 1943–1962.* Chicago, 1966.

17 BRANDES, Joseph. *Herbert Hoover and Economic Diplomacy. Department of Commerce Policy, 1921–1928.* Pittsburgh, 1962.

18 COOPER, R. N. *The Economics of Interdependence: Economic Policy in the Atlantic Community.* New York, 1968.

19 CURZON, Gerard. *Multilateral Commercial Diplomacy—The General Agreement on Tariffs and Trade and Its Impact on National Commercial Policies and Techniques.* London, 1965.

20 FANNING, L. M. *Foreign Oil and the Free World.* New York, 1954.

1 FEIS, Herbert. *The Diplomacy of the Dollar: First Era 1919–1932.* Baltimore, 1950.†

2 GIBB, G. S., and E. H. KNOWLTON. *History of Standard Oil Company (New Jersey), The Resurgent Years.* See 43.11.

3 GILBERT, M., and P. D. DICKENS. *Export Prices and Export Cartels (Webb-Pomerene Associations).* Monograph 6, Temporary National Economic Committee (TNEC). Washington, D.C., 1940.

4 GRISWOLD, A. W. *The Far Eastern Policy of the United States.*† See 38.3.

5 HOWLAND, C. P. "Mexico and the United States." *Survey of American Foreign Relations, 1931.* New Haven, Conn., 1931, pp. 1–29.

6 HOWLAND, C. P., ed. "The Caribbean." *Survey of American Foreign Relations, 1929.* New Haven, Conn., 1929, pp. 1–319.

7 HOWLAND, C. P., ed. "The New Pacific." *Survey of American Foreign Relations, 1930.* New Haven, Conn., 1930, pp. 1–341.

8 HOWLAND, C. P., ed. "The United States as an Economic Power." *Survey of American Foreign Relations, 1928.* New Haven, Conn., 1928, pp. 149–227.

9 KOTTMAN, R. N. *Reciprocity and the North Atlantic Triangle, 1932–1938.* Ithaca, N.Y., 1968.

10 LAWRENCE, S. A. *United States Merchant Shipping Policies and Politics.* Washington, D.C., 1966.

11 LINK, Arthur. *Wilson: The New Freedom.* Princeton, 1956, pp. 277–416.†

12 LINK, Arthur. *Wilson: The Struggle for Neutrality, 1914–1915.* Princeton, 1960, pp. 232–266, 456–550.

13 LINK, Arthur. *Wilson: Confusion and Crisis, 1915–1916.* Princeton, 1964, pp. 195–221, 280–318.

14 LINK, Arthur. *Wilson: Campaigns for Progressivism and Peace, 1916–1917.* Princeton, 1963, pp. 120–123, 328–339.

15 LIPSEY, R. E. *Price and Quantity Trends in the Foreign Trade of the United States.* See 3.11.

16 Mc CAIN, William L. *The United States and the Republic of Panama.* Durham, N.C., 1937.

17 NEVINS, Allan. *Herbert H. Lehman and His Era.* New York, 1963.

18 NOURSE, E. G. *American Agriculture and the European Market.* New York, 1924.

19 PARRINI, C. P. *Heir to Empire: United States Economic Diplomacy. 1916–1923.* Pittsburgh, 1969.

20 PATTERSON, Gardner. *Discrimination in International Trade. The Policy Issues, 1915–1965.* Princeton, 1966.

21 RIPPY, J. F. *Latin America and the Industrial Age.* See 40.16.

1   RIPPY, J. F. *The United States and Mexico*. See 40.17.

2   SCHATTSCHNEIDER, E. E. *Politics, Pressures, and the Tariff*. New York, 1935.

3   SCHEIBER, H. N. "World War I as Entrepreneural Opportunity: Willard Straight and the American International Corporation." *Pol Sci Q*, LXXXIV (1969), 486–511.

4   SIMON, M., and D. E. NOVACK. "Some Dimensions of the American Commercial Invasion of Europe, 1871–1914: An Introductory Essay." *J Econ Hist*, XXIV (1964), 591–605.

5   SMITH, R. F. "Formation and Development of the International Bankers Committee on Mexico." *J Econ Hist*, XXIII (1963), 574–586.

6   TASCA, H. J. *The Reciprocal Trade Policy of the United States*. Philadelphia, 1938.

7   TURLINGTON, E. W. *Mexico and Her Foreign Creditors*. See 40.21.

8   United States, Department of Agriculture. *Farmer's World. The Yearbook of Agriculture, 1964*. Washington, D. C., 1965, pp. 314–584.

9   United States, Tariff Commission. "Operation of the Trade Agreements Program, June 1934 to April 1948." *Reports*, 2d ser., No. 160. Washington, D.C., 1948.

10 WALKER, H. "Dispute Settlement: The Chicken War." *Am J Int Law*, LVIII (1964), 671–685.

11 WILLIAMS, W. A. *The Tragedy of American Diplomacy*. New York, 1959, pp. 45–60, 91–118, 148–183.†

12 WILTZ, J. E. *In Search of Peace: The Senate Munitions Inquiry*. Baton Rouge, 1963.

13 ZEIS, P. M. *American Shipping Policy*. 2d ed. Princeton, 1946.

NOTES

INDEX

INDEX

INDEX

INDEX

INDEX

INDEX

INDEX